Why Can't They Be Like Us?

Facts and Fallacies About Ethnic Differences
And Group Conflicts in America

By **ANDREW M. GREELEY**
Program Director
National Opinion Research Center
University of Chicago

Foreword by **ROBERT C. WOOD**
Director, Joint Center for Urban Studies
of MIT and Harvard University

INSTITUTE OF HUMAN RELATIONS PRESS
PAMPHLET SERIES
NUMBER 12

Institute of Human Relations Press
A. M. Sonnabend Memorial

The Institute of Human Relations Press publishes
books and pamphlets of original scholarship and research which cast light on intergroup attitudes, problems of prejudice and discrimination, and the status
of human rights here and abroad.

This is one of a series of publications dedicated to the
memory of A. M. Sonnabend, twelfth president of the
American Jewish Committee.

Why Can't They Be Like Us?
Facts and Fallacies About Ethnic Differences
And Group Conflicts in America

By ANDREW M. GREELEY
Program Director
National Opinion Research Center
University of Chicago

Foreword by ROBERT C. WOOD
Director, Joint Center for Urban Studies
of MIT and Harvard University
Head, Department of Political Science,
Massachusetts Institute of Technology

INSTITUTE OF HUMAN RELATIONS PRESS
The American Jewish Committee
165 East 56 Street, New York, N.Y. 10022

Edited and produced
by the PUBLICATIONS SERVICE
of the AMERICAN JEWISH COMMITTEE
SONYA F. KAUFER, *Director*

Library of Congress Catalog Card Number: 73-81091

Contents

For Pat Moynihan — the last of the old ethnics or maybe the first of the new ones:

May the ancient saints of Erin — Patrick, Brigid, Columkille and all the rest — continue to smile upon him.

About the Author

THE REV. ANDREW M. GREELEY, PH.D., is Program Director of the National Opinion Research Center at the University of Chicago, and a Lecturer in the University's Department of Sociology. He is Associate Editor of the *Review of Religious Research*, and a member of the editorial board of *Sociological Analysis*. He also serves on the Planning Committee of the 1969 National Conference on Higher Education.

Father Greeley has written more than a dozen books on the sociology of religion and religious education, including *Religion and Career: A Study of College Graduates* (1963); *The Education of Catholic Americans* (with Peter H. Rossi, 1966); *The Catholic Experience: An Interpretation of the History of American Catholicism* (1967); *The Student in Higher Education* (Report of the Hazen Committee, 1968); and *What Do We Believe?* (with Martin E. Marty and Stuart E. Rosenberg, 1968). He also writes a syndicated column for the Catholic press.

Acknowledgments

This booklet grew out of a paper given at the National Consultation on Ethnic America, which took place in June 1968. The Consultation, initiated by the American Jewish Committee and held at Fordham University, was co-sponsored by the American Council for Nationalities Service, the Foundation for Voluntary Service, the International Union of Electrical Workers, the National Catholic Conference for Interracial Justice and the Social Action Department of the United States Catholic Conference. I am grateful to Irving M. Levine and Judith Magidson of the AJC for encouraging me to develop the paper into a booklet.

My thinking on ethnic groups has been notably influenced by the most subtle Florentine since Niccolò Machiavelli — Peter H. Rossi — to whom my debt for ethnicity (though not for everything else I owe him) is hereby noted. Daniel P. Moynihan has consistently encouraged my interest in ethnicity and by both word and being persuaded me that ethnicity still lives. Norman M. Bradburn, the director of NORC, who is not an ethnic (but says he feels like one whenever I am around), has facilitated my interest in the subject, and my colleague, Galen Gockel, who definitely is an ethnic, provided me with some fascinating tabulations. Nella Siefert, who may or may not be an ethnic, typed the manuscript with her usual persistent care.

Foreword

"From many, one" — peoples as well as states — has been the glory of the American Republic, and its torment. In the beginning, the New World offered its bounty to the curious, the lucky and the brave, whatever their social status or nationality. The colonists impressed upon their sons: "You're as good as any man and better than none." The accident of Revolutionary history, pitting Englishmen against Englishmen, eliminated any possibility of claiming nationhood on the grounds of common race, culture or language, and forced us to accept the doctrine of "unalienable rights" — for all except the Negro slave.

We were pushed into the melting pot; but group identity persisted. Indeed, it powerfully buttressed the individual personality in a volatile, atomistic society dedicated, in principle, to the natural capabilities of the single citizen, the productive force of the single entrepreneur and the determining judgment of the single consumer. Kith, kin and kind still sustain us all amid the rigorous demands our economic and political systems impose upon us. They provide ritualistic, customary, traditional ways of making decisions that would be unbearably agonizing if each of us had to make them unguided and alone.

But the freedom which a nation of minorities encourages, and the richness in taste and style which group variety ensures, can torment both person and country, and place particular stress and tension on public institutions. The traditions of family and group do not reinforce, naturally and easily, the substance and style of government. Frequently, one set of traditions works against the other. Thus the schools are charged with the task of Americanization, while the family reinforces old ties and former loyalties. Thus government champions fair housing for all citizens, against the dictates of the market place and the desires of many residents. The concept of the melting pot is peculiarly a political one, designed to define citizenship and promote political consensus; it does not define individual activity. Our political ideology often rubs harshly against our private notions of how social and economic affairs should be ordered. Citizenship does not resolve the pains and dilemmas of a nation of ethnics.

In this book, Father Greeley manages to remind us of that pain — and nonetheless to comfort us. Combining the insight of the most "ethnic" of all Americans, the Irish priest, with the professional skills of the social scientist, he provides definitions, concepts and statistics that define the essentials of the contemporary ethnic condition. Clearly and reliably, he takes us through an estimate of the current situation, acknowledging our difficulties yet remaining confident of our capability to manage them.

In distinguishing between cultural and structural assimilation, marshalling evidence from such diverse sources as stratified polls and debutante balls, and suggesting that there may be a process of development common to all ethnic groups, Father Greeley offers conceptions and theories that may help us cope with the next decade of American politics. One does not have to subscribe to each of his generalizations to recognize the major contribution which he has made in these pages.

If I were to elaborate on only one of the principal points that follow from Father Greeley's presentation, it would be on the interplay between group tension and sensible politics. Quite possibly, tensions among ethnic groups could be accommodated and ultimately reduced by careful anticipation, mediation and planning. Quite possibly, some level of continuing hostility within the community is tolerable, is perhaps even a spur to timely change. Nevertheless, the effort and energy expended in dealing with such outbreaks detract from the other side of American political reality: the effective execution of public programs necessary to the urban world.

As long as government, especially local government, dealt only with relatively unimportant affairs, it could serve as a major vehicle for assimilation. Particular ethnic groups could take over bureaucracies and organize and control neighborhoods through ward politics. The price paid for such accommodation — in mediocre services, in graft, in corruption and in affronts to Anglo-Saxon morality — was bearable.

Today, the consequences of poor performance in education, renewal, pollution control or public safety are considerably more serious. A Model Cities program, for example, cannot remain indefinitely in the "planning process" while its political domination is under debate. Actual, discernible change — in jobs, houses, schools, parks, police — has to occur before discontent and disillusionment have a chance to set in.

So the task this generation faces in continuing our ethnic tradition is perhaps more difficult than before. On one hand, Afro-Americans labor under special circumstances, as identified by Father Greeley, and their problems in remedying the injustices brought about by our collective indecencies — as well as our problems in responding to these efforts — are likely to make their acculturation a tortuous process. On the other hand, the losses which urban society sustains as political institutions strive for accommodation are graver than formerly. We cannot as easily tolerate a lowering of professional standards when present levels of performance scarcely keep our highly technological society going.

It is urgent, then, that we face directly, honestly, vigorously the challenge in ethnic relations today. That challenge to our open society has never been greater, but the need to meet it has never been more imperative for the country and the world.

ROBERT C. WOOD
Director, Joint Center for Urban Studies of MIT and Harvard University
Head, Department of Political Science, Massachusetts Institute of Technology

April 1969

INTRODUCTION

WHEN THIS manuscript was first begun, teachers in New York City were involved in the third strike of the academic year, and the school children of New York City had had two months of extra vacation which they may have welcomed, but about which their parents and the political leaders in the city and the state were anything but enthusiastic. The causes of that strike were many and complex, and all are not really pertinent to this volume. But one way of looking at the conflict is to see it as a struggle between trade unionists, mostly but not entirely Jewish, determined to defend the traditional rights of union members won through many hard decades of strikes and collective bargaining, and black militant leaders and followers, determined to have control over what is taught in the schools their children attend and who teaches in these schools. While the press may have softened somewhat the ethnic nature of this conflict, one had only to watch the brief television interviews with either side to realize that most of the names and the faces and the accents on one side were Jewish and on the other side black.

The schools are now open, but the issue is far from settled. Two American ethnic groups previously thought to be allied are suddenly involved in fierce combat; at issue is power and, unfortunately, the amount of power available is limited or presumed to be limited. If the blacks are to have the power they want over decentralized school systems, then the United Federation of Teachers with its heavy component of Jewish membership is, in all likelihood, going to lose power. But it is not merely a battle between black educators and Jewish teachers that threatens Ocean

Hill-Brownsville and other areas of New York City; the blacks want more control over their local affairs, and the only way they will get more control, many of them feel, is to take it away from the dominant ethnic group in the situation — an ethnic group which happens to be Jewish.

Thus, American Jews, easily the most liberal and progressive ethnic group in the country, have found themselves faced with the possibility of grim battle with another ethnic group toward whom they have traditionally felt very sympathetic, and on whose side they have been in many other controversies. The Jew could fight the Irishman (and vice versa) with something of a clear conscience, but to fight the black is something else again. Yet, Jewish religious and civic leaders, for the first time perhaps, have discovered that there is somewhat more racism latent in the rank and file members of their communities than they would have thought and, at the same time, certain black leaders who were scarcely unaware of the anti-Semitism of some of their followers, now have found it convenient indirectly to appeal to these feelings in time of controversy and crisis.

I do not cite the New York school strike because I think I know a solution, or because I want to make a moral judgment about which side is right.[1] I cite the teachers' strike for a number of quite different reasons:

First of all, even though the blacks and the Jews are more than ethnic groups, the former being a racial group and the other a religious group, their conflict in Brooklyn is cut from the mold of a typical American inter-ethnic conflict. An older, more established and more powerful immigrant group is faced with the demands for increased power from a new, militant and very determined immigrant group. These conflicts are part of the history of American society, and particularly of American cities, and if the truth be told, show no signs of ending.

Thus, the example of the New York teachers' strike as an ethnic conflict will indicate how the term "ethnic group" will be used in these pages. For all practical purposes, we can equate ethnic group with immigrant group — though I hope to clarify the terms somewhat as I go along. Since even the American Indians were immigrant groups to this continent, we are quite clearly, as the late President Kennedy said, a nation of immigrants; and many, if not most, of the group conflicts that occur in the United States can be interpreted as a struggle between immigrant groups for what they think is their fair share of power in the society. These immigrant groups may also be racial or religious groups, and the racial and religious overtones of the conflicts make them even more serious; but it seems to me that the basic social dynamic at the root of ethnic conflicts is the struggle of immigrant groups for political and social power.

Secondly, the Ocean Hill-Brownsville battle ought to indicate, if proof were necessary, that there is no pair of ethnic groups which cannot, given the proper circumstances, lock horns with each other. It would have been inconceivable to many people a decade ago that there could be ethnic conflict between Jews and blacks. When Norman Podhoretz, the editor of *Commentary*, wrote an article a few years back bravely exploring the possibility of anti-Negro prejudice among Jews, the outraged reaction of many Jewish readers showed how unthinkable such conflict was considered. Yet the raw material of such a confrontation was already present, for there were two very large immigrant groups coexisting in the same geographical location, one possessing a great deal of socioeconomic and political power and the other possessing very little. The astute observer — and Podhoretz was certainly one — would have suspected that, should the weaker group seek to improve its position, conflict was almost inevitable.

My third point in citing the New York teachers' strike is that the political leadership and the social planners who determine on school decentralization seem to have been completely unaware of the hornets' nest they were stirring up. Yet anyone who had spent much time studying American ethnic groups would have been quite capable of warning political leaders and the social planners that they might be getting into very deep trouble, and that it would

[3]

be wise to prepare for it. And, as a matter of fact, a number of trained behavioral scientists did sound such warnings; but they were obviously not taken seriously.

It is no criticism of Mayor Lindsay's administration to say that a Democratic leadership might have been a little less likely to make the same mistake, for the Democratic party, founded as it is in the art of balancing ethnic communities one against another, has always had to be more aware of the realities of ethnic communities than has the Republican party. Indeed, the secret of Irish control of many American cities is that they are the most adept at playing the role of broker among other ethnic groups.[2]

It is an extraordinarily curious phenomenon that even though the United States is a nation of immigrants, and even though we have the most developed social sciences in the world, we have devoted relatively little attention to the ethnic groups which still flourish in our society. Later we shall suggest some possible explanations for this phenomenon, and yet the puzzle remains: why don't we know more about American ethnic groups?

One suspects that when the social historians of, let us say, the 23rd or 24th century look back on the era that we now presume to describe as the modern world, they will find two or three social phenomena of extraordinary interest. One, certainly, is the demographic revolution — the astonishing increase in the population level of the world that has occurred in the past century and a half. The second will be the westernization and industrialization of the non-Western world. And the third, unless I miss my guess, will be the formation of a new nation on the North American continent made up of wildly different nationality groups. The historians of the future will find it hard to believe it could have happened that English, Scotch, and Welsh, Irish, Germans, Italians, and Poles, Africans, Indians, both Eastern and Western, Frenchmen, Spaniards, Finns, Swedes, Lebanese, Danes, Armenians, Croatians, Slovenians, Greeks, and Luxembourgers, Chinese, Japanese, Filipinos and Puerto Ricans would come together to form a nation that not only would survive, but, all things considered, survive

[4]

reasonably well. I further suspect that the historians of the future will be astonished that American sociologists, the product of this gathering in of the nations, could stand in the midst of such an astonishing social phenomenon and take it so much for granted that they would not bother to study it.

They will find it especially astonishing in light of the fact that ethnic differences, even in the second half of the 20th century, proved far more important than differences in philosophy or economic system. Men who would not die for a premise or a dogma or a division of labor would more or less cheerfully die for a difference rooted in ethnic origins. Chinese and Malay fight each other in Southeast Asia; Ibo and Hausa in Nigeria; Greek and Turk on Cyprus; Czech and Slovak in Czechoslovakia; Arab and Jew in the Middle East; black (at least so-called) fights white (at least relatively) in the United States;[3] and the French and the English, running out of colonial peoples with which to contend, now renew the feud that the Hundred Years' War never did settle. Finally, along the lines of the Shamrock curtain, another feud simmers, and Frank O'Connor's immortal words, spoken from the secure position of his own agnosticism, are as true as ever: "The north of Ireland contains the best Protestants in the world and the south of Ireland the best Catholics, and there is nary a single Christian in the whole lot."

Immigration, Acculturation, Assimilation

Fashions in thinking, both popular and scholarly, about ethnic groups have changed. It was first assumed that the cultural forces of American society, particularly as applied in the public school system, would rather shortly level the differences among American immigrant groups and that most of the immigrants would, in effect, become good white Anglo-Saxon Protestants, speaking what Professor Peter Rossi[4] once labeled "radio-standard English." Even though the naive "melting pot" notion has long since lost its scholarly respectability, it is still, one suspects, a latent but powerful influence in American society. As members of older immigrant

[5]

groups say of members of younger immigrant groups, "Why don't they act like us?"

More recently, the idea of "cultural pluralism" emerged, which saw the United States not only as a nation of immigrants, but as a nation of immigrant groups; the immigrants, it was explained, would become American and thoroughly American, but at the same time retain much that was distinctive and creative about their own cultural heritage, perhaps even including their own language. A good deal of romantic prose has been written about how one nation is formed out of many, and about how Poles, Armenians, Italians, Jews, Irish, Hungarians and any other ethnic group one cares to mention can retain their own traditions and still be thoroughly and completely American.

Somewhere between the melting pot and cultural pluralism is the notion of the "multiple melting pot," first advanced by Ruby Joe Reeves Kennedy[5] and made popular by Will Herberg.[6] In this view the old immigrant groups were collapsing, but three super-ethnic groups based on religion were replacing them. One would, therefore, no longer think of oneself as German or Swedish or Irish or Romanian, but rather as Protestant, Catholic, or Jew.

A more sophisticated social science approach has been developed recently under the influence of S. N. Eisenstadt[7] and Milton Gordon,[8] who hypothesize two kinds of assimilation: cultural assimilation or acculturation, which involves the process of the immigrant group learning the manners and the style of a new society, and structural assimilation (or simply assimilation) in which the members of the immigrant group relate to members of other groups, particularly on the intimate levels of friendship and family formation, without any regard to ethnic differences. Eisenstadt and Gordon suggest that acculturation is taking place among immigrant groups, but not assimilation. Irish, Polish, Jews, blacks, Armenians, Romanians, Greeks, and so on, dress in the same kind of clothes, read the same magazines, watch the same television shows, perform the same kinds of jobs, share the same kinds of political and social values, but still, to a very considerable extent,

[6]

seek their intimate friends and their marriage partners from within their own ethnic group. According to this theory, acculturation can go on at a relatively rapid rate, and even create a certain pressure for assimilation without making assimilation anywhere near complete, and therefore ethnic groups continue to survive and probably will do so for the foreseeable future. This assimilation-acculturation view seems to combine the best perspective of both the melting-pot and the cultural pluralism approaches, but this does not necessarily mean that it is the best possible explanation for what's going on.

Another suggestion is found, however implicitly, in the excellent books written by Daniel Patrick Moynihan and Nathan Glazer[9] and Herbert Gans.[10] These writers tend to view ethnic groups as essentially interest groups, which came into being because of common origin and cultural background and continue in existence as the most appropriate units through which their members can seek greater political, social and economic power for themselves. Their assumption is that cultural differences among ethnic groups are declining rapidly, if they have not already been eliminated, and that it is the common interest in political and socioeconomic power which keeps the groups together.

There is nowhere near enough empirical data to make any confident assertions about the validity of the various approaches described above. Nevertheless, my colleague Peter Rossi and I are inclined to view the last two described with some reservation. We do not want to deny that the ethnic communities are very powerful interest groups; nor that acculturation seems to be going on at a faster rate than assimilation. But we are still forced to wonder why common national origin would be the basis for organizing and sustaining an interest group, and we would also wonder whether even acculturation has gone on quite as rapidly as some observers might think. To say, for example, that blacks and Swedes and Armenians share the same values is to speak a truism, at least up to a point; but anyone who has dealt with the three groups is well aware that in addition to the commonality of values, there is great diversity across these three groups — a diversity which may not be so great as to tear the fabric of American society apart, but is great enough to make them different kinds of communities.

In other words, we are not ready to assume that vast cultural differences do not persist. Our suspicion — and given the present state of the data, it is little more than suspicion — is that the core of these differences has to do with different expectations about close relatives; that is, in one ethnic group the expectations of how a husband or a wife, a father or a mother, a brother or a sister, a cousin, an aunt, or an uncle should behave are likely to be quite different than in another ethnic group. There is enough legend about Jewish mothers and Irish mothers for us to be able to realize that the expectations of these two ethnic groups, while in some sense quite similar, are also very, very different. But if we throw into the discussion the somewhat less known expectations of how a Missouri Synod German Lutheran mother ought to behave, we become quite conscious of how complex the question of the survival of ethnic differences really is.

The question is made even more complex by the fact that the various immigrant groups came here at different times, both in the development of the society they left behind and in the development of American society.[11]

European Origins and American Experience

As Nathan Glazer has pointed out, the Germans came from a society that was a nation long before it had become a state, and many of the German immigrants saw no reason why they could not create a German nation in the midst of the American continent (and as part of the American Republic). The Irish were not so inclined to create an Irish nation, although on one occasion they did attempt to invade Canada to take it away from England. But both these groups came quite conscious of their nationality, and quite capable of setting up ethnic enclaves, whether in rural Iowa or urban Boston (the Germans chose the country far more than did the Irish), that were based on the concept of nationality.

[8]

The second type of immigrant group, according to Glazer, was the Scandinavians who indeed came from states, but states that were not yet nations; for the Scandinavian peasants saw themselves less as members of nations than citizens of villages or members of a religious community. The Norwegians and the Swedes came to think of themselves as Norwegians and Swedes only when they banded together here to form communities of their fellows, particularly in the rural areas where the Scandinavians tended to settle. Glazer observed that it was easier for the Swedes and Norwegians, who had less of a notion of nationality than the Irish, to create nationality enclaves, because the Irish were in the city and the Swedes and Norwegians were in the country. In Glazer's words,[12] "We can, I think, conclude that where these early immigrants were isolated and remained rural, they showed an amazing persistence in maintaining the old language, religion, and culture. . . . For those . . . in the cities . . . a shorter time sufficed to remove the language and culture they had brought with them."

Glazer observes that among more recent immigrants, there are large numbers of people who came from nations struggling to become states (Poles, Lithuanians, Slovaks, Croatians, Slovenians), or from states struggling to become nations (Italy and Turkey and Greece), as well as from areas outside these Western concepts (Syrians), and of course one group — the Jews — who fit appropriately into none of these state-nation categories. "The newcomers became nations in America," Glazer points out quite succinctly; and he quotes with approval the insight of Max Ascoli, "They became Americans before they ever were Italians."

In two remarkable paragraphs, Glazer describes the astonishing phenomenon of the emergence of European "nations" in the American environment.[13]

> . . . Indeed, the effort of creating a national language, a task which the Western European nations had accomplished centuries before, was considerably facilitated for these Eastern peoples by American emigration. The coming together in American cities of people of various villages speaking various dialects required the creation of a common language, understood by all. The first newspaper in the Lithuanian language was

published in this country, not in Lithuania. The urbanization of many East European peoples occurred in America, not in Europe, and the effects of urbanization, its breaking down of local variation, its creation of some common denominator of nationality, its replacement of the subideological feelings of villagers with a variety of modern ideologies—these effects, all significant in making the East European peoples nations, were in large measure first displayed among them here in America. The Erse revival began in Boston, and the nation of Czechoslovakia was launched at a meeting in Pittsburgh. And all this should not surprise us too much when we realize that some European areas were so depopulated that the numbers of immigrants and their descendants in America sometimes equaled or surpassed those who were left behind.

If nations like Czechoslovakia were in large measure created here in America, other immigrants were to discover in coming to America that they had left nations behind—nations in which they had had no part at home. Thus, the American relatives of Southern Italians (to whom, as Ignazio Silone and Carlo Levi describe them, the Ethiopian war meant nothing more than another affliction visited upon them by the alien government of the North) became Italian patriots in America, supporting here the war to which they would have been indifferent at home.

We will turn later to the question of whether the ethnic groups whose history we have so briefly summarized will continue to survive in American society. Glazer is inclined to think that in the long run they will not, but that will be a very long run. My own inclination, after reading his extraordinarily insightful and instructive article, would be to think, rather, the opposite. America's ethnic groups are rooted only very partially in the European pre-immigrant experience, and have been shaped to a very great extent, however differentially for different groups, by the American experience. Glazer is quite right in saying that the Italo-Americans are very different from the Italo-Italians, and I can testify from personal experience that while the Irish-Irish and the American-Irish are in some respects similar, they are also very different. But this does not mean that American-Irish are about to become indistinguishable from American-Italians.

The ethnic group in this perspective is a combination of European cultural background, American acculturation experience (different for different groups), and political, social and eco-

[10]

nomic common interest. Not merely do different origins produce cultural differences; the different experiences in America reinforce the old differences and create new ones. The Kennedy administration was, one supposes, quite different from the administration of Sean Lynch in Dublin, but it is also very different from a WASP administration in this country, or the kind of administration we will have when finally Americans get around to electing a Jewish president.

There are a number of reasons why intensive study of American ethnic groups is long overdue. First of all, as we pointed out earlier, the wandering of the nations which has produced the United States of America is one of the most extraordinary social phenomena in the whole history of mankind. It provides us with a marvelous laboratory for the study of human relationships. What is there, precisely, in presumed common origin that attracts us to others of similar origin and repels us from those of different origins? Ethnic interaction and conflict in American society can tell us many things about human relationships that we are only beginning to dimly understand.

Secondly, our society faces immediate social problems which cannot be solved unless we understand more about the operation of the ethnic factor. I need not look at the statistics to be summarized later in these pages about Polish attitudes on racial questions to know that there is an acute problem in the relationship between Poles and blacks — at least one need not look at statistical tables if one lives in Chicago. Nor, if one lives in New York City, is it possible any longer to be unaware of the tension between Jews and blacks. If we understood more about how ethnic groups relate with one another, we might have some insights which would enable us to mitigate, if not eliminate, the dangerous tensions which threaten to tear apart our large cities.

Finally, it might be easier to understand the problems of the new immigrant groups if we were somewhat more aware of how older immigrant groups coped with their problems at a similar state in the acculturation process. I certainly do not want to subscribe to any interpretation of American racial problems which says that the blacks are just like any other ethnic immigrant group, and that their problems will be solved in the same way as the problems of the Irish or the Slovaks or the Italians or the Jews. For however degrading were the life conditions of the early white immigrants, they were at least not brought here as slaves nor kept in slavery or near-slavery for several hundred years. Nor are their skins a different color from that of other Americans. The combination of the slavery-serfdom experience and the difference in skin color (which, whether we liberals like it or not, still seems to be a universal human problem) puts the blacks at a much more serious disadvantage in acculturating to American society and obtaining their full rights than any previous group.

Nevertheless, there are certain similarities in the process through which all immigrant groups must pass in American society, and if we keep in mind that these are similarities and not exact identities, we can find them very illuminating. For example, there is, to my knowledge, not a single accusation that has been made by whites against American blacks that was not previously made against my Irish ancestors, with the possible exception that while blacks are accused of a high addiction to narcotics, the Irish were accused of an undue consumption of John Barleycorn. It was said of both groups that they were shiftless, irresponsible, pleasure-loving, violent, incapable of learning American ways, culturally inferior, too emotional religiously, and immoral (as proven by the high crime rates in their districts). The only basic difference that I can determine is that when the Irish rioted, they really did so in a big way. Nothing the blacks have yet done compares with — let us say — the anti-draft riots of 1863 in New York. Similarly, when the Irish engaged in guerrilla warfare, they were far more ruthless and effective; the blacks have not yet, thank God, tried to match the Molly McGuires.[14]

Finally, one may also study ethnic groups simply because they are interesting, and because, of all the branches of social science, the study of ethnic groups generates more amusing stories (that

[12]

are not pejorative to anyone) than any other branch of the discipline. Presumably American society needs all the humor it can get at the present time; within American society there is no segment more in need of laughter than the social sciences. But I wouldn't count on much laughter being tolerated there yet.[15]

NOTES

1. My personal inclinations are to side with the unionists and to say that the black militants are going to have to face the fact that the rights of union members are so deeply ingrained in American culture that black people cannot claim to be immune from recognizing these rights.

2. It is unfashionable to say anything kind about Chicago's Mayor Daley, at least east of the Indiana border, but it is still worth noting that in the last Chicago election Daley was able to obtain the majority support of both the black and the Polish communities in Chicago, a political feat of rare skill. Given the stresses of the times, it is dubious whether Chicago would be at all governable unless its leadership were able to attain consensus from both of these groups. There may be other ways of obtaining such consensus than the Daley political style, but there is little evidence that his opposition possesses such skill.

3. An earlier and somewhat shorter version of this material appeared in the international journal, *Concilium*, Vol. 4, No. 3, April 1967.

4. Professor Rossi was for many years Director of the National Opinion Research Center at the University of Chicago, and is now Chairman of the sociology department at Johns Hopkins University.

5. Ruby Jo Reeves Kennedy, "Single or Triple Melting Pot? Intermarriage Trends in New Haven," *American Journal of Sociology*, 49 (January 1944), pp. 331-39.

6. Will Herberg, *Protestant-Catholic-Jew* (New York: Doubleday, 1955).

7. S. N. Eisenstadt, *Essays on Comparative Social Change* (New York: Wiley, 1965).

8. Milton Gordon, *Assimilation in American Life* (New York: Oxford University Press, 1964).

9. Daniel Patrick Moynihan and Nathan Glazer, *Beyond the Melting Pot: The Negroes, Puerto Ricans, Jews, Italians and Irish of New York City* (Cambridge: Harvard and MIT University Press, 1963).

10. Herbert Gans, *Urban Villagers* (Glencoe, Ill.: The Free Press, 1962).

11. In this section I lean heavily on an article by Nathan Glazer: "Ethnic Groups in America," which is part of the symposium, *Freedom and Control*

[13]

in Modern Society, by Morroe Berger, Theodore Abel, and Charles H. Page (New York: Van Nostrand, 1954).

12. Nathan Glazer, *op. cit.*, p. 165.

13. Nathan Glazer, *op. cit.*, pp. 166-67.

14. The best way to assure oneself a steady stream of hate mail is to make these assertions to an audience that contains a fair number of the sons of St. Patrick. Usually the letters begin with, "And you a priest!" and conclude with references to how generous the Irish were to the Catholic Church, or with obscene references to the presumed sexual immorality of blacks. Generally, too, the writers will include some remark about how the Irish had to work for what they got, while the blacks are unwilling to work. My own presumption is that both Irish and blacks, like any other ethnic group, have similar proportions of compulsive workers and compulsive loafers. Anyone who thinks that all the Irish earned their living is unaware of the masterful skill of Irish political leaders in days gone by in keeping the shiftless and indolent alive through the use of political payrolls. And in certain cities, these activities have not yet ceased.

15. I was recently asked to give a paper at a university symposium on the sociology of religion and the sociology of knowledge. Given the composition of my audience and the perfectly valid assumption that few of them knew very much about Mannheim or Marx, I decided to concentrate more on the sociology of religion than on the sociology of knowledge, facetiously explaining at the outset that one reason for this was that the ideas in the sociology of knowledge were expressed in heavily Teutonic prose which ran through my Celtic intellect much as Gale Sayres runs through defensive secondaries. The laughter in the audience indicated that virtually everyone understood my point, and also realized that I was being critical neither of Celts nor of Teutons. Nonetheless, two solemn commentators who were appointed to make remarks about my paper sternly took me to task for making pejorative ethnic comparisons. I suppose I was lucky to get away without being criticized for being anti-black, because I compared Gale Sayres with Teutons, or the largely black defensive secondaries to Celts.

WHAT IS AN ETHNIC?

IT IS very difficult to speak precisely about what an ethnic group is, but it is possible to develop a working definition somewhat empirically and to describe ethnicity by showing how contemporary ethnic groups came into existence. While, as I indicated earlier, there is some broad equation possible between ethnic groups and immigrant groups, it is not enough merely to say that the ethnic groups are immigrant groups. Whatever definition we emerge with is likely to leave us with some very embarrassing questions. For example: Does everyone belong to an ethnic group? Is a white Anglo-Saxon Protestant an ethnic? Are Texans or Kentuckians, for example, ethnics? And what about American intellectuals, particularly those who are not Jewish and who seem to be quite cut off from any trace of nationality background? Do they constitute a new ethnic group? Such questions do not admit of quick answers; yet we must address ourselves to them if only because there are a number of Americans who are not prepared to take ethnic issues seriously unless responses to those questions are provided.

The ancestors of the immigrants to the United States were, for the most part, peasants living in the agricultural communities of European post-feudal society. This society was post-feudal in the sense that the peasants either owned some land of their own, or at least had been emancipated from the worst rigors of the feudal system. The peasant villages of Ireland, Germany, Italy, Poland or the Balkans were not the most comfortable places in the world, and the nostalgia bordering on romance over them that is to be found in the works of some 19th-century sociological writers is misleading. Granted that post-feudal peasant society provided a great deal of stability, it did so at the price of stagnancy; and granted also that it provided a great deal of social support, it did so by imposing a great deal of social control. A man was, indeed, sure of who he was and where he stood and what he might become in such societies, but most men were in inferior positions and had no expectation of becoming anything more than inferior.

Nevertheless, there was a warmth and intimacy and closeness in these peasant communities. A person could be sure of the pattern of relationships and be sure that while he might have enemies, he also had friends, and the friends and enemies were defined by historic tradition. Society indeed controlled individual members, but it also rallied support, strength and resources when help was needed. It was a highly personal world, not in the sense that the dignity of the human person was respected more than it is today, but in the sense that relationships were, for the most part, between persons who knew each other, understood their respective roles, and knew what kind of behavior to expect. Family, church and community were all fairly simple and overwhelmingly important, and though mankind had evolved beyond the all-pervading intimacy of the tribe or the clan, life was nonetheless quite personal and intimate in a stylized and highly structured way.

Some time after 1800, European peasant society began to break up, partly because, as the population increased, there were more people than jobs in the agricultural communes, and partly because the emergent industrialization in the cities desperately needed new labor. Those who made the move from commune to metropolis in hope of finding a better life began a number of social trends which actually meant a better life, if not for them, at least for their children or their grandchildren. The pilgrimage from peasant village to city, and later to the cities of America, brought to many the wealth of the affluent society.

But something was also lost: the warmth and intimacy, the social support of the commune was gone. Gabriel Le Bras, the famous French sociologist of religion, remarked that there was a certain

[16]

railroad station in Paris which apparently had magical powers, because any Breton immigrant who passed through that station never set foot in a Catholic church again. The church, the family, the commune which had provided the parameters of the ordinary person's life were all either destroyed or so substantially altered as to be unrecognizable. The peasant migrant was forced to spend most of his waking day with people who were strangers. This is an experience which does not seem peculiar to us at all, but to a man who had encountered few strangers ever before in his life, it was frightening and disorienting.

"Our Own Kind"

In the strangeness of the new environment, the individual or his battered and bedraggled family looked around for someone with whom he had something in common — hopefully a place in the big city where previous migrants from his village had settled. Because such settlers were "his kind of people," he could trust them; they knew their obligations to him and would help him to adjust to this new world in which he found himself. Thus, in the Italian neighborhoods of New York's lower east side in the early 1920's it was possible to trace, block by block, not only the region in Italy but also the very villages from which the inhabitants had come. Indeed, it is no exaggeration to say that some of these blocks were nothing more than foreign colonies of Sicilian villages.

If you weren't able to find someone from your own village, then you searched for someone from your area of the country; even though you may never have met him before, you could depend on him to have some of the same values you had, and you shared some sort of common origin. He may not have been from Palermo, but at least he was a Sicilian; he may not have been from Ballyhaunis, but at least he was from County Mayo; and these village or regional groupings, based especially on family and kinship relationships, in their turn sought protection and some power against the strange world in which they found themselves by banding together, one with another. So that for many groups, as

Glazer has pointed out, the nationality became a relevant factor only when the necessities of adjusting to American experience forced the village and regional groups to band together.

The ethnic group provided a pool of preferred associates for the intimate areas of life. It was perhaps necessary in large corporate structures to interact with whomever the random possibilities of the economic system put at the next workbench or desk. But when it came to choosing a wife, a poker (and later on, bridge) partner, a precinct captain, a doctor, a lawyer, a real estate broker, a construction contractor, a clergyman and, later on, a psychiatrist, a person was likely to feel much more at ease if he could choose "my kind of people."

So then, as Max Weber[1] defines it, an ethnic group is a human collectivity based on an assumption of common origin, real or imaginary; and E. K. Francis, supplementing the Weber definition, has argued that the ethnic collectivity represents an attempt on the part of men to keep alive, in their pilgrimage from peasant village to industrial metropolis, some of the diffuse, descriptive, particularistic modes of behavior that were common in the past. The ethnic group was created only when the peasant commune broke up, and was essentially an attempt to keep some of the values, some of the informality, some of the support, some of the intimacy of the communal life in the midst of an impersonal, formalistic, rationalized, urban, industrial society.

That the immigrants tried to associate with their own kind was understandable enough in the early phases of immigration, but we are still faced with the necessity of explaining why ethnic groups have persisted as important collectivities long after the immigration trauma receded into the background. Why was not social class the membership around which American city dwellers could rally, as it was in England? Why have the trade unions rarely, if ever, played quite the fraternal role in American society that they have in many continental societies? Granted that urban man needed something to provide him with some sort of identification between his family and the impersonal metropolis, why did

[18]

he stick with the ethnic group when there were other groupings to which he could make a strong emotional commitment?

First of all, one must acknowledge the fact that other groups have, on occasion, provided the same enthusiasm that ethnic groups do. Some men need more of this enthusiasm than others, and by no means all who need it seek it in a nationality group. As a matter of fact, it is probably likely that for many, at least at the present stage of acculturation, religion is more important than ethnicity as a means of social definition and social support, a means of identifying ourselves in relation to others. However, religion and ethnicity are so intertwined in the United States that it is extremely difficult to separate them; an attempt to sort out this relationship is one of the major challenges facing social theorists who become concerned with ethnic groups.

Pluralism and Group Survival

It seems to me that there were two factors which made for the survival of ethnic communities after the immigration trauma was over. First of all, the United States is a society which has demonstrated considerable ability in coping with religious and racial pluralism, one way or another. A nation which was, in effect, religiously pluralistic before it became politically pluralistic, the United States had to learn a sufficient amount of tolerance for religious diversity merely to survive. It was necessary only to expand this tolerance when the new immigrant groups arrived on the scene with their own peculiar kinds of religious difference. It also seems that, even before the Revolutionary War, nationality differences were important, so the Germans and the Irish (usually meaning the Scotch Irish) were considered as a group quite distinct from the Anglo-Saxon majority. Furthermore, even though the racial relationship had deteriorated into tyranny and slavery, there was, at least until the invention of the cotton gin, apparently some possibility that even this might be peacefully settled. In other words, by the time the large waves of immigrants came, in the early and middle 19th century, America was already acquiring some skills in coping with the religiously and ethnically pluralistic society. The immigrants were not welcome, and considerable pressure was put upon them to become Anglo-Saxons as quickly as possible. Yet the pressures stopped short of being absolute; the American ethos forced society to tolerate religious and ethnic diversity even if it did not particularly like it. Under such circumstances, it was possible for the ethnic groups to continue and to develop an ideology which said they could be Irish, German, Polish or Jewish, and at the same time be as good Americans as anyone else — if not better.[2]

But why is it still important to be an Italian, an Irishman, a German or a Jew? Part of the reason, I suspect, has something to do with the intimate relationship between ethnicity and religion. But another element, or perhaps another aspect of the same element, is that presumed common origin as a norm for defining "we" against "they" seems to touch on something basic and primordial in the human psyche, and that, as we pointed out in the previous chapter, much of the conflict and strife that persists in the modern world is rooted in such differences. If anything, the separatist nationalisms within the major nation states seem stronger today than they were a quarter of a century ago: Catholics rioting in Londonderry, Ireland; Scots electing nationalist members to Parliament; the mutterings of Welsh separatism. The Basques, and even the Catalonians, grumble about being part of Spain; the Flemings and the Walloons are at odds with each other over Louvain; the Bretons wonder if it might be possible for them to escape from France; and the French Canadians are not at all sure they want to remain part of the Canadian nation, even if they could have their own prime minister.

Most of these separatist movements make little sense in terms of economic reality. The Province of Quebec would be hard put to go it on its own; Wales and Scotland would very quickly have to form a political and economic union with England, not much different from the one that already exists; and Brittany would have to do the same with the government in Paris. Maybe tribal loyalties and tribal separatism ought not to continue in a rational, industrial world — but they do, and it is a threat to the fabric of almost any society large enough to be made up of different ethnic communities. One is almost tempted to say that if there are no differences supposedly rooted in common origin by which people can distinguish themselves from others, they will create such differences. I suspect, for example, that if Scotland did become independent of England, there would be conflict between the Highlanders and the Lowlanders as to who would run the country. Ethnic diversity seems to be something that man grimly hangs on to, despite overwhelming evidence that he ought to give it up.

Edward Shils has called these ties primordial and suggests that, rooted as they are with a sense of "blood and land," they are the result of a pre-rational intuition. Such an assumption seems to make considerable sense, but is difficult to prove empirically. It is certainly true, however, that family, land and common cultural heritage have always been terribly important to human beings, and suspicion of anyone who is strange or different seems also to be deeply rooted in the human experience. Ethnic groups continue, in this hypothesis, because they are a manifestation of man's deep-seated inclination to seek out those in whose veins he thinks flows the same blood as flows in his own. When blood is also seen as something intimately related to belief, and both blood and belief impinge strongly on what happens to a man, his wife and his children, he is only too ready to fight to protect the purity of that belief, or the purity of his blood, or the purity of his family when it is threatened by some strange outside invader.

This view of ethnicity, it must be confessed, is essentially a negative one. But one can make a more positive case for it. It could be said that the apparent inclination of men, or at least of many men, to consort with those who, they assume, have the same origins they do, provides diversity in the larger society and also creates sub-structures within that society that meet many functions the larger society would be hard put to service. And while the demons of suspicion and distrust prove very hard to exorcise from

[21]

inter-ethnic relationships, such suspicion and distrust are not, I am convinced, inevitable. If they can be eliminated, ethnicity enriches the culture and reinforces the social structure.

To sum up, ethnic groups have emerged in this country because members of the various immigrant groups have tried to preserve something of the intimacy and familiarity of the peasant village during the transition into urban industrial living. These groups have persisted after the immigrant experience both because American society was not basically hostile to their persistence and because of an apparently very powerful drive in man toward associating with those who, he believes, possess the same blood and the same beliefs he does. The inclination toward such homogeneous groupings simultaneously enriches the culture, provides for diversity within the social structure, and considerably increases the potential for conflict. It may some day be possible to isolate ethnicity from suspicion and distrust, but no one has yet figured out the formula for doing so.

NOTES

1. Max Weber, "The Ethnic Group," in Talcott Parsons, et al. *Theories of Society*, Vol. 1, p. 305 (Glencoe, Ill.: The Free Press, 1961).

2. Daniel Patrick Moynihan summarized the super-patriot syndrome beautifully when he said, "At last the time had come to investigate Harvard men, and Fordham men were going to do the investigating."

THE FUNCTIONS OF ETHNICITY

BEFORE WE TURN to the role of ethnic groups in contemporary American society, we must face some of the insistent questions that were raised in the previous chapter.

First of all, is everyone an ethnic? In one sense, of course, the answer to such a question is an obvious yes. It is true that all our ancestors at one time did migrate to the American continent. But does national origin seem important to everyone? Here the response must be no. For some people ethnic background is very meaningful both because it affects their behavior and is an important part of their self-definition. For others, ethnic identification may be completely unimportant and ethnic background may have little influence on their behavior. In other words, ethnicity is one of a number of ways in which Americans may identify themselves and which they may use as part of their self-definition. At the social-psychological level, then, not everyone is an ethnic. But the relevant question seems to be — under what sets of circumstances do which people express what sort of ethnic identification? When is ethnicity relevant, and for whom? Unfortunately, American behavioral science cannot answer that question at the present time.

One suspects, however, that ethnicity becomes very important in three sets of circumstances: 1) When an ethnic group is very large and has great actual or potential political and economic power. It is probably far more meaningful to say that someone in Chicago is Polish than to say that Senator Muskie of Maine is Polish. And to be Irish probably means much more in Boston than it does in Tallahassee, Florida. 2) When one is a member of a small but highly visible or well-organized minority. To be Mexican, or black or Jewish is probably always important, because these background characteristics are almost always highly visible. 3) When a sophisticated group suddenly becomes conscious that it has become a minority and is surrounded by many other well-organized ethnic communities. Thus, to be a white Anglo-Saxon Protestant in, let us say, Nebraska may not be nearly as meaningful as to be the same thing in New York City, when one suddenly discovers that one is, indeed, a member of a minority group — and a minority group which, for all its economic power and social prestige, enjoys (or at least enjoyed, until recently) very little in the way of political potential. Visibility, sudden recognition of minority status, or being a large group in an environment where ethnic affiliation is deemed important — these three variables may considerably enhance social-psychological and social-organizational influence of ethnic groups.

In such a framework it can probably be said that to be an intellectual or an academician is not to be a member of an ethnic group, although academia may serve as a functional substitute for an ethnic group. Thus, someone who leaves behind, somewhat regretfully, the warmth and social support that he felt in his family and neighborhood as he grew up, may find some substitute in being part of the intellectual community. This quest is made even more complex by the fact that the intellectual community is heavily Jewish in composition, and that the degree of identification with the Jewish ethnic group varies considerably among Jewish intellectuals. One solution that many gentile intellectuals finally settle for is to begin to think of themselves as quasi-Jewish.

Perhaps the most critical issue that can be raised about ethnic groups is the nature of their relationship to religious groups. Will Herberg's answer was simple enough — the ethnic groups are dissolving into the super-ethnic community provided by one of the three major American religious groupings. But it is apparent that Herberg was somewhat premature in his judgment. To be a Norwegian Protestant is by no means the same as to be a Southern Baptist; nor is it the same as to be a Missouri Synod Lutheran.

[24]

Similarly, Irish Catholicism and Polish Catholicism are very different phenomena and provide very different kinds of identification. The mutual resentment between Poles and Irish is, in many instances, far more serious than are their feelings toward any of the heretics, schismatics, infidels, agnostics and apostates (all currently called separated brothers) outside the Church. The lines among the various Catholic ethnic groups may be growing a bit more blurred, but they are still there, and any bishop who forgets it and sends an Irish priest to a Polish parish, or vice versa, is not going to be able to forget it for very long.

I would make two assertions about the relationship between religion and ethnicity.

1) The ethnic groups provide subdivisions and subdefinitions within the various religious communities. Catholicism is, for example, still too big a category to be completely satisfactory — at least for everyone — as a quasi-communal identification.

2) There is a two-way flow of influence between religion and ethnicity. From one point of view it can truly be said that the Irish are Catholic because they are Irish. That is, the identification of Catholicism with Irish nationalism — the biggest favor that Mother England ever did for the Catholic Church — has helped to make the Irish the strong, if not to say militant, Catholics that they are. On the other hand, the fact that the Irish in the United States are Catholic and are linked to the Catholic Church through the Irish tradition probably makes them more likely to be conscious of their Irish origins than they would be if religion and ethnicity were not so intimately linked in their cultural experience. Whether it is religion or ethnicity that is celebrated during the St. Patrick's Day parade is anyone's guess, but I think we can say, with some degree of safety, that it is both, and that the nature of the relationships and of the mix between the relationships is likely to vary from individual to individual.

Ethnic groups — even if they are not sub-cultures (and I suspect they are) — are at least sub-structures of the larger society, and in some cities, comprehensive sub-structures. The Polish community in Chicago, for example; the Jewish community in New York; the Irish community in Boston; the black community of Harlem all represent a pool of preferred associates so vast and so variegated that it is possible, if one chooses, to live almost entirely within the bounds of the community. One can work with, play with, marry, attend church with, vote with and join fraternal organizations with people who are of exactly the same ethnic background. One can choose fellow ethnics to perform all the professional functions one requires, from interior decorator to psychiatrist to undertaker. One can belong to ethnic organizations, read ethnic newspapers, seek counsel from ethnic clergymen, play on ethnic baseball teams and vote for ethnic candidates in elections. While some of us may lament the exclusiveness in such ethnic communities, it is nonetheless true that the pattern of ethnic relationships constitutes an important part of the fabric of the larger community, organizing the amorphous population of the city into a number of clearly identifiable and elaborately structured sub-groups.

Sub-Structures and Life Styles

From the viewpoint of those responsible for the larger social structure, these organizations are particularly convenient because the leadership is readily identifiable and is generally willing to negotiate for the advantage its own community members with an eye on the political realities in which it finds itself. (In Los Angeles, for example, citizens of different ethnic backgrounds are not organized into ethnic communities, and this is one reason Los Angeles is quite ungovernable. In Chicago, on the other hand, it is the ethnic sub-structures that make it still possible — though difficult — to govern.)

These same sub-structures also provide a greater degree of stability in personal and professional relationships, because those who are one's "own kind of people" are considered to be substantially more trustworthy and may, in fact, actually be more trustworthy than the members of out-groups. (By trustworthy here I do not mean that an Irish psychiatrist would cheat a German

[26]

client: I simply mean that a German psychiatrist might much more easily understand what his German client was talking about.)

Ethnic groups also serve as bearers of distinctive cultural reactions. Some of the research on the relationship between medicine and ethnicity, for instance, indicates that Italians are much more likely to give free expression to feelings of pain than are Irish, and thus are likely to be a considerable trial to hospital personnel. The Irish, on the other hand, bear their pain grimly and bravely and may cause less trouble, but it is harder to discover how sick an Irishman really is, because he's not likely to tell you.

There are also differences in political style. Professor James Q. Wilson, of the Department of Political Science at Harvard, reports that when an Irish police officer has a choice between formal, official channels of communication and informal, unofficial channels, he will almost always choose the latter. It was said of the Kennedy administration that, in addition to the titular head of the various administrative agencies, there was always someone at a slightly lower level who was "Kennedy's man" and had special contact with the White House on the affairs of that agency.

Some researchers have suggested that there is a great deal more fatalism and lack of achievement orientation among Italians than there is among white Anglo-Saxon Protestants. Blacks insist that "soul," and all the word implies in the black community, is not to be found among most white ethnic groups. And, as we shall point out in a later chapter, ethnic background also correlates strongly with occupational choice. Jews are more inclined to be doctors than anyone else, while Germans, both Protestant and Catholic, overchoose engineering careers and the Irish overchoose law, political science and, more recently, the foreign service.[1]

I would like to make two not altogether facetious suggestions for research. First of all, we might take a serious look at debutante balls. In a city like Chicago there is a complex and elaborate hierarchy of debutante cotillions. The most important and best publicized is the Passavant cotillion which is sponsored allegedly to support one of the city's famous hospitals. It is basically a debutante party for the Protestant aristocracy, though occasionally a Catholic girl may make it if her father is rich enough or important enough. (One of Mayor Daley's daughters was a Passavant deb.)

The second ranking cotillion, sponsored by the Irish Catholic aristocracy (although certain non-Irish Catholics are permitted into it in much the same fashion the Passavant cotillion tolerates an occasional Catholic), is known as the Presentation Ball, and is named after the presentation of the young ladies supposedly to the Chicago Archbishop or one of his hapless auxiliaries.

But then the fun begins. There are Polish, Czech, Slovak, Ukrainian, German (Protestant and Catholic), Scandinavian, Puerto Rican and black cotillions, and by no means just one for each ethnic community. In fact, a researcher eager to find the similarities and the differences in such critically important social events could well keep himself busy for weeks on end, were his stomach and his nervous system strong enough.

It would be easier, I suspect, to study the culture of wedding celebrations. On this subject I can claim to be somewhat more of an expert than on debutante balls, since for weal or woe I never was fortunate enough to make one of the latter, but at one time in my career I was required professionally to show up at an almost infinite number of weddings. My impressions, subject to confirmation or rejection by further research, were that Irish wedding receptions were marked by drinking (and eventually, frequently by singing); Polish receptions by endless dancing; Bohemian receptions by prodigious consumption of food; and Jewish receptions by much food, and prodigious and interminable conversation.

I cite these two areas for research not merely because there is a certain amount of humor in debutante balls and different kinds of wedding celebrations, but also because I suspect that they will strike a familiar chord in the reader's memory. It seems fairly obvious, even though we have little empirical data to confirm it, that the ethnic communities, particularly in areas where they are relevant for their members, do indeed maintain traditions of their own. What some of these traditions would mean to their cousins in the old country may perhaps be another matter. Whether the County Mayo or the County Clare Irish, for example, would make any sense out of the Presentation Ball seems highly questionable.

Mobility Pyramids and Mobility Traps

One final point needs to be made about the social functions of ethnic groups: They provide mobility pyramids that may turn into mobility traps.[2] Because the ethnic sub-community is, at least if it's big enough, a comprehensive sub-structure, it is possible for an upwardly mobile professional and businessman to build his career almost entirely within its confines. Not only a general practitioner, but even a surgeon, can have patients almost all of his own ethnic background; a Catholic academician can achieve a position within the system of Catholic colleges (which are, for the most part, Irish Catholic colleges) that he would not enjoy in the larger academic system; a political leader can gain far more power as the head of an ethnic faction within the party than he would if he tried to operate without such a power base; a contractor or an undertaker may do very well indeed servicing the needs of his ethnic colleagues, where he might be considerably less successful competing beyond the bounds of the ethnic group; even a racketeer, though he may be viewed with contempt by the larger society, may be respected for his success and affluence within his own sub-structure.

These mobility pyramids are, of course, very helpful for those who manage to achieve influence, affluence and prestige that might well be less possible for them in the larger society. And such substructural mobility probably adds to the satisfaction and morale of the members of an ethnic community. On the other hand, there is the risk of a mobility trap. A promising academician who accepts his first major appointment at a Catholic college may move up very rapidly within the Catholic system, but find the door closed to him for more meaningful mobility outside the system. Similarly, a doctor who has built his clientele within the ethnic community may feel that he has great prestige there, but when he goes to medical association meetings and finds himself outside the

[29]

power elite of these associations, he may wonder if he might not have had even greater success beyond his own ethnic group.

A few individuals manage to avoid the ethnic trap, moving from positions within their own group to similar positions in the larger structure, with increased influence and prestige. Thus, certain journalists whose careers originally were established within Catholic publishing journals have been able, because of their success on these journals, to switch over to important positions with secular newspapers and magazines. And the Kennedys, whose power roots lie in the ward politics of Boston, were able — with the aid of large sums of money and great personal dedication — to break out of the Irish Catholic political mold and make it in the big time. But the mobility pitfalls persist, and many ethnics eager for upward mobility are faced with Caesar's choice — whether to be first in the small pyramid or run the risk of being second (or much lower than second) in Rome.

In summary, then, the functions of ethnic groups in American society are multiple. They keep cultural traditions alive, provide us with preferred associates, help organize the social structure, offer opportunities for mobility and success, and enable men to identify themselves in the face of the threatening chaos of a large and impersonal society. On the other hand, they reinforce exclusiveness, suspicion and distrust, and, as we have already noted, serve as ideal foci for conflict. Finally, ethnic groups are something like the Rocky Mountains or the Atlantic Ocean — whether we like them or not really doesn't matter very much; they are concrete realities with which we must cope, and condemning or praising them is a waste of time.

NOTES

1. A finding which suggests that the Irish may have left behind the precinct for the Embassy. Whether this be social progress or not is beyond the competencies of this writer to judge.

2. In this section I lean heavily on the suggestions of Peter H. Rossi and the writings of Norbert Wiley.

[30]

STEPS IN ETHNIC ASSIMILATION

ANYONE who is interested in peace and tranquillity within American society has wondered if inter-ethnic peace in the United States is possible. Before we turn to this thorny question, however, we must face yet another complex of American life — the fact that the various ethnic groups which coexist with one another are at different stages in the process of acculturating and assimilating into the American environment.

Let me outline, briefly, a progression which may help us to understand something of this acculturation process. There are, as I see them, six steps in this process: 1) culture shock; 2) organization and emergent self-consciousness; 3) assimilation of the elite; 4) militancy; 5) self-hatred and anti-militancy; and 6) emerging adjustment.

Phase 1. Cultural shock: In the first phase, the immigrant group has just arrived in the host society. The patterns of behavior that were established in the Old World are jolted and jarred. The old culture is felt to be under savage attack and the members of the immigrant group are frightened and disorganized. The leaders, such as they are, are not sure that they can hold their people together, and the outside society keeps up a drumfire of criticism. Almost all the newcomers are poor, and they work (when they find work) at the most menial and poorly paid tasks. (This was the plight, for example, of the Irish arriving in New York and Boston after the great famine, of the East European Jews arriving in New York at the turn of the century, of the blacks arriving in the cities of the North after the First and Second World Wars, and of the Poles arriving in Chicago at the time they were studied by W. I.

Thomas and Florian Znaniecki in 1918.) Sheer survival is the only issue.

Phase 2. Organization and emerging self-consciousness: In the second phase, the immigrant group begins to become organized; its clergy, its precinct captains, the leaders of its fraternal organizations, its journalists, become the key figures in the communities. The immigrants are learning the language and their children are becoming "Hibernicized" in the public schools (or if one happens to be Catholic, in the Irish Catholic schools). The newcomers are clawing their way up the economic ladder and becoming semi-skilled, occasionally even skilled, workers. Some of the brighter young people are embarking on professional careers. Having survived the first trauma of integration, the elite of the community now become concerned about whether that which is distinctively theirs is going to be lost in the assimilation process. The language, the culture, the religion of the Old World must somehow be preserved — although almost everyone agrees that the group must also become American. There is not much leisure and not much money, but enough for self-consciousness and ethnic pride to begin to assert themselves, and the political leaders of the community become skilled in bargaining for concessions in return.

Phase 3. Assimilation of the elite: In the third phase of the acculturation process, ambivalence begins to emerge. The immigrant group has managed to climb at least partially into the lower middle class. Its members are storekeepers, artisans, skilled workers, clerks, policemen, firemen, transit workers and militant trade unionists. Money is scrimped and saved to provide for the college education of promising young men, and even of young women, who are expected to become schoolteachers. The group's pride increases; though it is still diffident toward the world outside, there is a tinge of resentment and anger beneath the diffidence. "We may be struggling to win acceptance," they say under their breath, "but some day you'll have to bargain with us on *our* terms."

At the same time, the more talented and gifted individuals begin to break out of the ethnic mobility pyramids and find their way

[32]

into the mainstream. Those who make it find it very difficult not to be ashamed of their ethnic background. (Such writers, for example, as James T. Farrell and John O'Hara demonstrate this tense social awkwardness about their own minority relationship to the intellectuals of the University of Chicago and of the eastern Protestant aristocracy.) There simply are not enough others of their own background who have also made it for the ethnic arriviste to feel at ease. No longer a part of that from which he came, neither is he fully accepted by those among whom he has arrived — on the contrary, he may occasionally find himself displayed as an interesting objet d'art.

The degree of assimilation and alienation of elites at this stage varies from group to group, even from person to person. The Kennedy clan, for example, was more or less accepted by the Harvard aristocracy and the international cafe society of "beautiful people"; yet it does not seem they were totally at ease in these worlds. But neither were they totally South Boston Irish; as a matter of fact, some of the most vicious criticisms of the Kennedys I have ever heard have come from Boston Irish clergymen who view the clan as somehow unfaithful to their Boston Irish roots.

Phase 4. Militancy: In the fourth phase, the immigrant group has become fully middle class and even edges toward upper middle class. It now is thoroughly, and at times violently, militant. It has sources of power; it has built up a comprehensive middle culture; it does not need the larger society (or so it thinks), and wants as little to do with it as possible. Its members are warned of the dangers of associating with the larger society, and simultaneously are urged to become better at everything that society does.

This is the time when a comprehensive structure of organizations is developed duplicating everything that exists in the larger society. Thus, American Catholicism has generated a Catholic lawyers' guild, a Catholic physicians' guild, Catholic sociological, historical, and psychological societies, Catholic hospital wings, and indeed, Catholic versions of just about everything else to be found in the American culture. It is also the time of super-patri-

[33]

otism, when the immigrant group tries to prove it is not only as American as any other group, but more so. (This is when Moynihan's Fordham men begin to investigate the WASP Harvard men.)

The successful immigrant group now throws its power around with little regard for the rights and feelings of others. "We were pushed around when we were powerless," its members argue, "now we're going to push back. It *was* their city, it's now *our* city, and we will run it our way, whether they like it or not." In the first three phases the immigrant group was the object of constant rejection; this rejection has been at least partially internalized, and now the group is over-compensating. It is busily demonstrating not only to the world outside, but also (especially) to itself that it is not inferior, and it is demonstrating this noisily, aggressively and uncompromisingly. Suspicion and distrust of the larger society and noisy, highly selective pride in the accomplishments of one's fellow ethnics are the order of the day. It is at this stage, one must note, that the ethnic group is most difficult to deal with and most likely to engage in conflict with other ethnic groups.[1]

Phase 5. Self-hatred and anti-militancy: In the fifth phase, the ethnic group is generating a substantial upper middle and professional class. Its young people are going to college in larger numbers and many are becoming successful and economically well-integrated members of the larger society. There is no question, as in the case of the earlier elites, of these new and much larger elites' alienating themselves from the immigrant group; but from the perspective of full-fledged members of the larger society, they are acutely embarrassed by the militancy, the narrowness, the provincialism of their own past, and by the leaderships of organizations which seem to have a vested interest in keeping that past alive. Self-hatred, latent in the first three phases and hidden behind militancy in the fourth phase, finally comes out in the fifth phase, and devastating criticism is aimed at almost every aspect of one's own tradition and almost every institution which strives to keep one's culture alive. Yet, for most of the self-critics, there is no thought of abandoning the ethnic community or its culture

[34]

completely. There are intense, emphatic demands for drastic and immediate modernization — demands which cannot possibly be met — and intense ambivalence toward the ethnic group. The self-critics cannot live with their ethnic background, and they cannot live without it.

Phase 6. *Emerging adjustment:* Finally, in the sixth phase, another generation appears on the scene, securely upper middle class in its experience and equally secure in its ability to become part even of the upper class. Such a generation is quite conscious of its ethnic origin; it does not feel ashamed of it and has no desire to run from it, but neither is it willing to become militantly aggressive over its ethnicity. It cannot understand the militant defensiveness of the fourth phase or the militant self-hatred of the fifth, and sees no reason in theory or practice why it cannot be part of the larger society and still loyal to its own traditions. It is in this phase, one suspects, that Hansen's Law ("what the father forgets, the son remembers") becomes operative. There is a strong interest in the cultural and artistic background of one's ethnic tradition. Trips are made to the old country, no longer to visit one's family and friends, but out of curiosity and sometimes amused compassion at how one's grandparents and great-grandparents lived. Many elements of the ethnic traditions survive, some on the level of high culture, some in a continuation of older role expectations. The younger members of the ethnic groups, indeed, delight over these differences which they find so "interesting" and so much fun to explain to friends and classmates of other ethnic groups.

It is about this time that the members of an ethnic group that has reached the top begin to wonder why other groups, which have not moved as far along, are so noisy, raucous and militant.

If one were forced to cite examples of, let us say, the last three phases, one might guess that the American blacks are moving into phase four (militancy), and that the more recent Catholic immigrant groups, such as the Italians and the Poles, are in the middle of phase four and beginning to move beyond it. Irish and German Catholics began to move into phase five (self-hatred) at the end of the Second World War and have been engaging in an orgy of self-criticism (what Father Edward Duff has called mass masochism) ever since (a self-criticism which has been made even more cynical and pessimistic by the revolution of the Second Vatican Council). My own impression is that some of the American Irish in their 20's are moving into phase six (adaptation), and that large numbers of American Jews under 40 are already in that phase.

Some Complicating Factors

The progression described above is quite clearly an oversimplification. It elevates hunches, impressions and occasional illustrations to the level of high theory. But at the present stage of our research on ethnicity, it is the best this writer can evolve, and perhaps it will stimulate others to try for something better.

Two observations and one warning might be added: First of all, the posture of a given ethnic group in relation to the other groups is likely to change dramatically as the group moves through the acculturation-assimilation process. It is probably impossible to accelerate the process very much, but at least one can understand it and realize why, at a given time, a particular ethnic group may be very difficult to deal with. It would be wise to realize that one's ancestors were equally difficult to deal with at a somewhat earlier period in history.

The second observation is that it is probably unwise for members of outside ethnic groups to become involved in the internal conflicts that plague a group through phases three, four and five. For outsiders to encourage one set of leaders in a group is the surest way in the world to make sure those leaders are disqualified from further effective leadership. There may never before have been so descriptive and emotionally charged a phrase as "Uncle Tom," but the idea is foreign to no ethnic group; and if there are leaders in a given community with whom we are better able to get along, we are well advised not to embarrass them by pointing them out to their fellows as the most sensible of men, because that will be the end of their power.

[36]

My warning has to do with the possibility of regression. If an ethnic group feels itself attacked again, after having "made it" in the larger society, it may very well regress, at least temporarily, to an earlier stage. It should not be surprising, therefore, that some rank and file members of the Jewish community in New York are likely to feel quite violent about the threat of black anti-Semitism. Their shock and displeasure are similar to the anger of the white Protestants as later immigrant groups displaced them — though the white Protestants generally did not go through the difficult and painful process of assimilating and acculturating to a society. Since it was their society to begin with, they did not have to pay the psychic price that later immigrant groups paid, and hence are not likely to be quite so angry when someone backs them into a corner.

This outline of the stages of acculturation and assimilation provides us with a tool, admittedly crude, for understanding many of the other intergroup conflicts which plague the United States, particularly in its large cities. It also enables us to make some tentative predictions and raise some interesting questions. One such question, for example, concerns the remarkable phenomenon of the Puerto Rican experience. Some students of Puerto Rican acculturation have suggested that it has taken place at a more rapid rate than that of any other group that has ever come to the United States; and while the Puerto Rican leadership has been militant, the community has rarely engaged in violence. It will be a very interesting community to watch as it moves into the final three phases we have described.

NOTE

1. As we shall note in a later chapter, hostile feelings seem to be increasing between Catholics and Jews, although both have presumably moved fairly well through the militancy phase. The sequence I have described does not exclude the possibility of regression.

COMPETITION AMONG ETHNIC GROUPS

IT IS NOW TIME for us to concentrate on the most critical aspect of ethnic life in the United States — competition among ethnic groups — though competition is by no means the sole cause of intergroup conflict. We must assume that competition among different groups for resources that are scarce or are presumed to be scarce, is inevitable. The question is whether, and to what extent, such competition can be kept from turning into conflict.

A number of social scientists, most notably Lewis Coser, have argued that social conflict is a good thing, that it is a safety valve permitting society or groups within it to let off excess steam which, if contained, could lead to violent explosions. Coser argues that when the patterns of relationships in society are no longer adequate to the social realities, group conflict is a way of forcing a restructuring without destroying the patterns completely. Thus, if a given ethnic group has less political power than its size, group-consciousness and desires would make appropriate, conflict between this group and other groups which have more power than their size seems to warrant, is a way of restructuring the social order before frustration and dissatisfaction tear it apart.

In the context of Coser's very wise theorizing, the present phase of black militancy can be seen as highly constructive for society, because it is forcing concessions to the blacks of positions, prestige, power, control and responsibility appropriate to their size, their stake in society and their emerging self-consciousness. If there were no social conflict to force this restructuring, there might be an eruption which would tear the total society apart. Although some black extremists use a rhetoric of destruction, it still seems

[38]

safe to say that, thus far, black militancy seems to have restructuring rather than destruction as its goal. Such a perspective is an extremely useful one; but it is still necessary to point out either that social conflict is useful up to a point and then itself becomes destructive of the social fabric, or that there are two kinds of social conflict — that which leads to restructuring, and that which leads to destruction. Unfortunately, the two shade off one into another in such a way that it's often hard to tell which kind we are watching.

The late John Courtney Murray wrote and spoke frequently of the "conspiracies" within American society. He argued that the various religious groups were, indeed, competing for power and influence, but at least within some vaguely agreed-upon "rules of the game" — rules which everyone was careful not to make too explicit lest the very explicitness become a source for conflict. Social conflict is likely to lead to restructuring as long as there is some agreement on the rules of the game, and it is likely to lead to destruction when there is not even a vague agreement. (Some of the student unrest currently afflicting the campuses seems to be operating in a context where one can see no agreement on the rules of the game between the student extremists and the rest of the university.) The non-violent phase of the civil rights movement operated under rather explicitly agreed upon rules of the game, and even though the non-violent phase is now asumed to be over, a substantial segment of the black leadership, in reality if not in rhetoric, still seems willing to settle, as did other ethnic groups before them, for "more" within the existing structure. On the other hand, the struggle between the black school districts and the white, largely Jewish teachers' union in New York seems to bode ill for the future of the city precisely because it springs from a disagreement on the rules of the game.

Arenas of Conflict

Most of the conflicts between ethnic and religio-ethnic groups currently going on in American society are well within the rules of the game (one is that we may accuse other groups of breaking the

[39]

rules, as long as we do not push that accusation too far). Violence may occasionally break out, especially between the races, and on the fringes where one ethnic ghetto brushes against another, either physically or psychologically. But given the size, complexity and newness of American society, the astonishing phenomenon is not that there is inter-ethnic conflict, but that it is not more destructive.

There is, first of all, the conflict of political competition. In New York, there is the struggle between Jews and Catholics for control of the Democratic party — a struggle which has led many Jews to form what is basically their own political party, the Liberals. And among the Catholics there is conflict between the Italians and the Irish for control of the Democratic Party. The Republican Party is still basically white Protestant, though it has managed to attract some liberal Jews who find the liberal and aristocratic WASP more to their liking than either the unsophisticated Catholics of the Democrats or the socialistically oriented Jews in the Liberal Party. The blacks and the Puerto Ricans are generally within the confines of the Democratic coalition, and have been accorded some positions of power and prestige, but nowhere in keeping with their numbers. The Republicans have managed to elect a white Protestant liberal as mayor of New York; and the intelligent and sophisticated Mr. Lindsay has attracted large support from both Jews and blacks in his challenge to the Italo-Hibernian-dominated Democratic party. For a native New Yorker, this all makes a great deal of sense in a bizarre way, and for a native Chicagoan like myself, it is very understandable (though we have a hard time grasping how the New York Irish can be as inept as they are; in Chicago we are much better at playing one ethnic group off against another). But one suspects that for the native of Nebraska or Nottingham or Naples or Nantes or Nijmegan, the politics of New York City (or Boston or Chicago or Detroit) must seem like an incredibly confused jungle. To them, all we can say is, you should see what it's like in Los Angeles.

The second focus for conflict is housing. As each ethnic group improves its economic situation, it seeks new housing — at least housing that is new for it — and begins to move from its original location into neighborhoods that previously have been the preserve of other ethnic groups. Generally speaking, the first neighborhoods to be so "invaded" are already declining, either out of physical obsolescence or because the most ambitious of its citizens are already seeking better housing for themselves. But invasion by a "foreign" ethnic group is a profound threat; not only does it imply (despite overwhelming evidence to the contrary) a decline in sales value of one's own house; it also is a challenge to friendship patterns, churches, familiar landscape and shopping areas, and all those things a man has come to value in that particular area he thinks of as his own.

The conflict between white and black has been so well publicized in recent years that we tend to forget that other ethnic groups have "battled" for neighborhoods, and that such conflicts continue, even today. When I was growing up on the west side of Chicago, an Italian family was only a little more welcome in an Irish neighborhood on the south side than a Negro family would have been; and while the replacement of Poles by Puerto Ricans in Chicago is more peaceful than the replacement of whites by blacks, there is still tension and potential conflict in such replacement of one ethnic group by another.

Education provides another focus for inter-ethnic conflict. Again the most obvious conflict today is between blacks and whites, over attempts to create racial balance in the public school system and the efforts of black militants to gain more and more control of the schools in their own communities (which means, in part, control over white teachers who work in these schools). But various white ethnic groups have fought among themselves for control of the public school system, with Catholics warring against Protestants and various Catholic groups fighting with each other. Catholics have generally supported religious activities in public schools (though Catholic liberals and intellectuals have opposed it); Protestants are divided on the issue and most Jews are for rigorous separation of church and state in the public schools. A similar

[41]

division takes place on state support of one sort or another to religious schools, though Protestant groups would shift somewhat more against such aid, and at least some Jews would be in favor of it. Finally, within the Catholic Church, the struggle continues between the dominant Irish and other groups for control of the Catholic school system, which the Irish have generally used as an Americanizing — that is to say, Hibernicizing — force, while other immigrant groups have attempted to develop their own national Catholic schools where their culture and language are kept alive.

Ethnic battles also rage in the trade unions, where leadership, once Irish or German or Jewish, has recently shifted somewhat toward the Italians and the Slavic immigrant groups. In the meantime, the blacks have become conscious that they are underrepresented at the middle and higher levels of union leadership and are beginning to demand what they deem to be adequate representation in the upper councils of labor.

In the business world, particularly the world of the small shop or the small entrepreneur, such as the construction contractor, vigorous, if not to say vicious and cut-throat, competition exists along ethnic lines, though there is little documentation on the subject. Similarly, in the demimonde of the rackets, Italian (which is to say generally Sicilian) leadership has replaced the Irish and the occasional Jewish leadership of years gone by, but now finds itself beginning to be threatened by restless black allies.

The Struggle for Power

Politics, housing, religion, education, unions, business — indeed in almost any area in American life where conflict is possible — the ethnic groups form temporary shifting alliances as their members struggle to obtain more power or to preserve the power they already have. Differences in religion and social class may exacerbate the conflict situations and the apparently inevitable human inclination to question the good faith of those who are different makes the conflict potential even worse. The suspicion, if not hatred, for example, of a Jewish or Protestant intellectual and liberal for the

[42]

Irish politician has by no means disappeared from the American scene. (While it is conveniently forgotten now how bitterly party-line American liberals criticized President Kennedy, it perhaps is not yet forgotten how *The New Republic* dismissed his younger brother as "pure Celt, arrogant and ruthless," a few days before his assassination.)

Hatred for that which is different apparently still lurks just beneath our civilized veneer. We are not yet that very far from the tribal state, and while necessity keeps most of us to the rules of the game, we are deeply suspicious that members of other groups will violate those rules at the first opportunity.

Some of the conflict situations we have mentioned are purely ethnic: for example, the struggle between the Irish and other nationality groups for control inside the Catholic Church, while other conflicts — black against white, Jew versus Catholic — are ethnic and racial or religious. While it is difficult in our present state of knowledge to sort out the influence of race, ethnicity and religion, it is not particularly important, for practical purposes, that we do so. But we must remember that it is not merely religious theory that keeps Catholics and Jews suspicious of each other, nor merely racial history that creates the problem in Ocean Hill-Brownsville. The struggle between Catholic and Jew over the public schools, for example, is not so much rooted in religious differences as in the political and social styles of two immigrant groups jockeying for prestige and power in an urban world where they are closely juxtaposed. Only if we understand that the battle is between two ethnic groups searching for more power themselves, but afraid to give the distrusted foe any more power lest he use it against them, can we understand the depth of the passions and fears involved.

Theoretical positions on civil rights made blacks and Jews close allies for a long time; but today they are often at odds. Yet, it is not racism that is the issue, save very indirectly. Rather, it is a struggle between two immigrant groups for what both think is their proper share of the urban power pie.

[43]

In both the Catholic-Jewish and the Negro-Jewish conflicts, of course, religion and race are involved in many different ways, but I am suggesting that even if these two factors could be drained out of the conflict, the basic resentment toward a group of "strangers" who are trying to take something from us, or keep something from us that is rightfully ours, will make the conflict almost as serious as it is at the present time.

"WE" AND "THEY": THE DIFFERENCES LINGER

WE NOW TURN from speculation and theory about ethnicity to some concrete data about differences among ethnic groups in America. Most of the findings I am about to cite have not yet been published, but I think they help establish the fact that we are not just idly speculating when we say that ethnic groups have survived in the United States, and continue to be the bearers of different cultural traditions. In addition, I think they may provide us with some hints as to the problems that ethnic differences seem to portend for American society, as well as some clues to further research that might be appropriate.

The data described stem from three major sources: first, a national survey of American Catholics[1] done in 1963; second, data about the attitudes of June 1961 college graduates seven years after graduation (collected as part of a long-term study of education and careers by the National Opinion Research Center of the University of Chicago);[2] and finally, information obtained from a study of urban neighborhoods undertaken in 1967, also by the National Opinion Research Center.

The tables documenting these findings are contained in an unpublished set of National Opinion Research Center data entitled *Information About American Ethnic Groups,* and the professional sociologist interested in inspecting these tables is welcome to do so. Since most readers, however, will not want to struggle through the statistics, only a few of the tables are reproduced here, while the most interesting and significant findings in all the data are summarized below.[3]

[45]

The 1963 Catholic Survey

From the 1963 survey (Table 1) we learn that the Irish, first ar-
rivals among American Catholics, are the most successful group
as measured by their education, as well as by the prestige of their
jobs[4] and their income. They also score highest on measures of
general knowledge, are the most open-minded and the most likely
to exhibit high morale, as gauged both by measures of happiness[5]
and of anomie, i.e., the state of disorientation, anxiety and isolation that develops when standards of conduct and belief have
weakened or disappeared. They are the most pious and least given
to religious extremism, racism[6] or anti-Semitism.[7]

The Catholic German Americans are almost as successful as the
Irish in occupational status, though not in education or income.
They are only slightly less devout than the Irish, slightly more

Table 1. SELECTED ATTRIBUTES
OF CATHOLIC ETHNIC GROUPS IN U.S.

	Irish	Germans	Italians	Poles	French
Have completed high school	77%	62%	51%	46%	42%
Hold prestige jobs	32	31	13	17	22
Earn over $14,000 a year	24	19	17	18	7
Belong to Democratic Party	70	65	67	77	70
Score high on general knowledge	18	9	7	3	5
Score high on open-mindedness	52	48	42	43	40
Consider themselves "very happy"	41	36	35	27	40
Score low on anomie	64	51	47	43	49
Score high on piety	32	31	13	30	22
Score high on religious extremism	19	20	24	34	28
Score high on racism	44	46	54	61	51
Score high on anti-Semitism	29	47	43	52	54
(Number of persons interviewed)	(328)	(361)	(370)	(184)	(177)

given to religious extremism, somewhat less secure in their personal morale and somewhat less open-minded.

Italians and Poles, both more recent Catholic immigrants, have yet to achieve the educational, occupational and financial success of their Irish and German predecessors, and score lower in happiness and open-mindedness. They score higher on measures of racism than the older groups, but while the Poles also score higher on anti-Semitism, the Italians are lower on anti-Semitism even than the Germans. Poles are most likely, and Italians (together with Germans) least likely, to be members of the Democratic Party. And whereas Italians are the least pious of all the Catholic groups, the Poles are almost as devout as the Irish.

Finally, French Americans[8] are among the least pious of American Catholic groups, second only to Poles with respect to religious extremism, and highest of all groups on measures of anti-Semitism. They score almost as high as the Irish in happiness, but they tend a good deal more toward anomie.

Can these differences be explained away, perhaps, by the fact that some of the Catholic ethnic groups have been in this country longer than others, or become better educated? The way to check this is to compare only individuals of the same generation and educational level — for example, those who are at least third-generation Americans and have completed high school (Table 2). We then find that the typical differences between ethnic groups tend to diminish, but that many of them persist at least in some degree.

Thus, in occupational prestige and income the Irish and Germans are still the most successful, though the Poles have just about pulled abreast. The Irish still rank highest in general knowledge, with Italians now in second place and Germans in third. The Italians now are even more likely than the Germans to have left the Democratic Party. Poles again score high on anti-Semitism and racism, and both Poles and Italians continue to score low on happiness. The Irish and French are again the happiest, putting to rest (forever, I hope) the notion that the Celts are a morose and melancholy lot. I shall leave to others to explain why the descend-

[47]

	Irish	*Germans*	*Italians*	*Poles*	*French*
Hold prestige jobs	31%	34%	12%	32%	21%
Work as professionals or managers	45	47	37	22	31
Earn over $14,000 a year	26	22	3	21	11
Belong to Democratic Party	67	61	51	62	76
Score high on general knowledge	26	17	20	11	9
Score high on open-mindedness	51	56	51	34	40
Consider themselves "very happy"	47	38	26	32	48
Score low on anomie	74	60	44	61	60
Score high on piety	32	32	10	20	39
Score high on religious extremism	14	15	20	31	26
Score high on racism	39	30	54	61	29
Score high on anti-Semitism	25	38	32	59	43
(Number of persons interviewed)	(131)	(102)	(29)	(24)	(31)

ants of sunny Italy seem so gloomy in this instance — though with only 29 of them in the table, one could easily argue that the whole sample must have been made up of sombre Milanese.

The findings of the 1963 survey were sorted out according to region as well as generation, with at least one striking result: The Poles' high scores on measures of anti-Semitism and racism were limited to the Midwest. Poles on the East Coast did not differ from other Catholics in these respects. It seems reasonable to conclude, therefore, that while ethnic differences persist even after three or four generations and among the better educated, the shape and direction of these differences is affected by various other factors — economic, social or geographical. In all likelihood, the heavier the concentration of an ethnic group in a given area, the more

[48]

likely it is to form a tight ethnic community and to take a negative attitude toward outsiders.

The Study of College Graduates

The National Opinion Research Center's study of June 1961 college graduates, and their attitudes seven years after graduation, was not limited to Catholics; hence it provides information about a substantial number of ethnic groups.

One of the factors touched on was political affiliations. According to the findings, Jews are most likely to belong to the Democratic Party, and Protestants least likely. Polish Jews are more likely to be Democrats than German Jews, and Irish Catholics are more likely to be Democrats than German or Italian Catholics.

The Jews and the Irish score as less likely than any other ethnic group to hold racist ideas, with the Scandinavians and the Poles just behind them. Other groups tend to be substantially more prejudiced, with the Protestant Germans ranking highest among the lot on measures of racism.[9]

As one might expect, Jews score higher on measures of reading and cultural interests than do Protestants, and Protestants score generally higher than Catholics — although Germans, both Protestant and Catholic, are the least likely to report intensive reading habits. German Jews seem to have more intense reading and cultural interests than Polish Jews; the Scandinavians lead the Protestants, and the Irish score highest among the Catholics. Polish Catholics, however, are most likely to plan a career in Academia, followed by German Jews, Protestant Scandinavians and Catholic Irish. Protestant and Catholic Germans, together with Italians, are least likely to plan academic careers.

The differences among the college graduates are, in their own way, even more striking than the differences among the general population; for the college graduates are all young, well educated and (one assumes) thoroughly American. And a college education does indeed seem to change some things — Polish attitudes toward blacks, for example, apparently improve very considerably as the result of higher education. Yet differences of 20 to 30 per-centage points persist in many other measurements of attitude and behavior, despite college training. Fifty-one per cent of the Catholic Irish were willing to agree with the Kerner Commission's conclusion that white racism was the cause of Negro riots in cities, for example, while only 34 per cent of their German coreligionists would vote the same way (Table 3). Thirty-seven per cent of the Protestant Scandinavians could accept the Kerner Commission's conclusions, but only 28 per cent of their German confreres were willing to agree with them.

Turning from racism to another measure of attitudes on con-temporary social problems, an index of sympathy with student militancy, we find a similar pattern. The Jews and the blacks are the most sympathetic; the Irish are the most sympathetic among the Catholics, but only slightly ahead of the Poles; and the Scan-dinavians are the most sympathetic of the Protestants — in fact, of all white Christians. Germans, both Catholic and Protestant, are the least sympathetic within their respective religious traditions.

Regional differences, or differences in the size of the localities in which the respondents live, may explain many of the differences reported here. Yet the geographical distribution of, let us say, the Irish Catholic, Italian Catholic and Polish Catholic population is

Table 3. RACIAL ATTITUDES AMONG COLLEGE GRADUATES OF DIFFERENT RELIGIOUS AND ETHNIC BACKGROUNDS
(June 1961 graduates, surveyed in 1968)

"White racism is the cause of Negro riots in the city"

	Proportion agreeing		Proportion agreeing
Blacks	84%	Catholic Italians	35%
German Jews	54	Catholic Germans	34
Catholic Irish	51	Protestant English	30
Polish Jews	43	Protestant Irish	28
Catholic Poles	43	Protestant Germans	28
Protestant Scandinavians	37		

such that region or locale cannot account for all of the differences. (Neither, of course, can social class, since all the respondents are college graduates.) The socialization experience of higher education has not eliminated ethnic group differences in attitudes and behavior, even among the Scandinavians and the Germans, whose geographic distribution is similar, or among the Irish, Italian and Polish Catholics, who share a common religion.

The Neighborhood Study

The 1967 study of urban neighborhoods indicates that there are considerable differences in neighborhood behavior among American groups. The findings show that Jews most often belong to neighborhood organizations and engage in a considerable amount of socializing, while the Poles score lowest on the socializing scale. Italians are least likely to belong to organizations (though they are most likely to describe themselves as very sociable). The Irish most frequently state that they enjoy everything in their neighborhood and worry little, while both the Italians and the Jews score high on measures of worry. But the Italians, while they admit to worrying, also claim more often than the Jews or any Protestants that they are enjoying themselves. It would seem, then, that the Irish and the Germans are low worriers and high enjoyers, while the Italians are high worriers and high enjoyers.

Perhaps the most significant findings in the neighborhood study have to do with where people live and how frequently they associate with members of their families (Table 4). Of all the ethnic groups Italians most often live in the same neighborhood as their parents and siblings and visit them every week; together with the Poles and French, they also live most frequently near their in-laws or see them weekly. Protestants as a group are less likely than Catholics to live in the same neighborhood with relatives and to visit them weekly. Jews, though no more likely than Protestants to live in the same neighborhoods, are more likely to visit their parents weekly than any of the Protestants, or the Irish and German Catholics.

Table 4. FAMILY RELATIONSHIPS
OF RELIGIOUS AND ETHNIC GROUPS

	Live in same neighborhood with			See weekly		
	Parents	Siblings	In-laws	Parents	Siblings	In-laws
Catholics						
Italians	40%	33%	24%	79%	61%	62%
Irish	17	16	16	49	48	48
Germans	10	13	10	48	31	41
Poles	29	25	24	65	46	53
French	15	23	24	61	41	62
Protestants						
English	19	13	12	39	26	35
Germans	12	13	14	44	32	39
Scandinavians	14	11	17	39	26	31
Jews	14	12	14	58	33	58

When the same data are sorted out according to social class and the physical distance that separates the respondents from parents and relatives, an extremely interesting finding emerges. Italians are still the most likely to visit both their parents and their siblings. The Jews are now in second place in visits to parents, but at the bottom of the list where visits to siblings are concerned. The Irish, on the other hand, are relatively low on the parent-visiting list, but right behind the Italians in visits to siblings. It would seem that the stereotypes of the tight Italian family, the dominating Jewish parent and the clannish Irish sib group are, at least to some extent, backed up by hard statistics.

Since relationships with parents and siblings play a major role in the formation of personality, it seems reasonable to suggest that the different patterns experienced by these three ethnic groups in the earliest years of life help make for quite different personality traits. If this be true, we can expect the subtle differences among the various ethnic groups to persist into the future.

Previous studies of Italian Americans, principally by Herbert Gans, indicate that the familial peer group — siblings and other relatives of one's own age — are the most important influence on lower-class Italians. To some extent, data in the surveys cited above confirm Gans' findings. The Italian's relationships with his parents seem to be a function of physical proximity; with his siblings, the bond overcomes even physical separation. However, Gans suggests that this sibling closeness is essentially working-class and not Italian behavior, whereas in our findings the ethnic differences seem to persist even when different social classes are examined separately.

An Overview

It is extremely difficult to tie together the diverse data from the various studies cited into a coherent pattern. But the information summarized above, together with some findings not quoted here, allow us to attempt the following generalizations:

The earlier immigrant groups are both the most socially successful and the most tolerant, but there are enough differences between, say, the Irish and the Germans, or between the Italians and the Poles, to suggest that other factors are at work besides the time at which one's parents washed up on American shores.

Of all the ethnic and religious groups the Jews are politically the most liberal and socially the most active, as well as economically the most successful. They are close to their parents, relatively less close to their siblings, and given to worrying.

Italians are conservative in their child-rearing practices and extremely close to their relatives — to their parents basically because they live close to them, but to their siblings, apparently, because the sibling relationship is very important to them. They are only moderately successful socially and economically, relatively uninvolved in organizational activity (perhaps because of their heavy family commitment) and liberal on some political questions, though more likely to leave the Democratic Party than are other Catholic ethnic groups. Though they think of themselves as very sociable, they are likely to have a lot of worries. They score rather low in measures of canonical religiousness, and fairly high on prejudice, though not as high as the Poles or the French.

[53]

A college education apparently reduces, but does not completely eliminate, these differences in degree of prejudice.

The Irish are economically and socially the most successful among Catholic immigrant groups and the most liberal politically and socially. They have very strong ties with their siblings, are the most devoutly Catholic, and the least prejudiced, and their view of themselves ranks them as the happiest and most self-confident.[10]

The Poles score lowest, economically and socially, of all Catholic immigrant groups, and those among them who live in the Midwest and have not graduated from college are the most likely to be prejudiced. They are very loyal to the Catholic Church (but in a more "ethnic" way than the Irish or the Germans). They are the most likely to be Democrats and, if they are college graduates, to be liberal Democrats. They are low in morale and sociability, and high on measures of anomie.

The many historical, sociological and psychological processes that are involved in producing these differences are still frustratingly obscure, but to me they constitute one of the most fascinating questions for social research still open in our culture.

NOTES

1. For a detailed discussion of the methodology of this survey, see *The Education of Catholic Americans* by Andrew M. Greeley and Peter H. Rossi (Chicago: Aldine, 1966).

2. The graduates were interviewed for the fifth time in the spring of 1968, under a grant from the Carnegie Commission on the Future of Higher Education.

3. Since the facts tread in the sensitive area of ethnic differences, a word of explanation is appropriate: The three studies cited were national sample surveys, carried out by the most careful professional methods. Although the number of respondents in each ethnic group may seem quite small to readers unfamiliar with survey research, they are, for the most part, large enough to provide some confidence that the respondents were representative of the total population. (Note carefully that the words I use are "some confidence," not absolute certainty.) The reader should be warned, however, that none of the surveys were done with ethnic research explicitly in mind. We are using questions that were designed for other purposes to seek out

information about American ethnic groups. No claim can be made that the differences reported are conclusive, nor that the speculations derived from the statistical tables are more than tentative. One wishes very much that better data were available.

4. "Prestige jobs," in this context, means jobs in categories 8 through 10 of the Duncan Occupational Scale. This scale divides American occupational groups into 10 categories according to their prestige as perceived by the total population.

5. The "happiness" measure is based on a classic survey research item which asks if respondents feel very happy, pretty happy or not too happy.

6. Racism was measured by asking respondents whether they agreed strongly, agreed somewhat, disagreed somewhat or disagreed strongly with the following statements: 1. "Negroes shouldn't push themselves where they are not wanted." 2. "White people have a right to live in an all-white neighborhood if they want to, and Negroes should respect that right." 3. "I would strongly disapprove if a Negro family moved next door to me." 4. "Negroes would be satisfied if it were not for a few people who stir up trouble." 5. "There is an obligation to work toward the end of racial segregation."

7. Anti-Semitism was measured by asking respondents whether they agreed strongly, agreed somewhat, disagreed somewhat or disagreed strongly with these statements: 1. "Jews have too much power in the United States." 2. "Jewish businessmen are about as honest as other businessmen."

8. Most of the "French" in the sample are French-Canadian Catholics from NORC's Manchester, New Hampshire, primary sampling unit.

9. I hope Polish critics of an earlier presentation of these data will note carefully my assertion that Poles who graduated from college in 1961 are considerably less likely to be prejudiced than many other American ethnics. Of the 10 ethnic groups under consideration in the college graduate study, the Poles ranked seventh in racist attitudes.

10. Embarrassed by the fact that the Irish group looks so "good" in these comparisons, I would like to go on record as saying, "There's a hell of a lot wrong with us, too."

THE FUTURE OF ETHNIC GROUPS

IT IS NOW TIME to address ourselves to three general questions: 1) Are ethnic groups likely to survive in American society? 2) Can anything be done to mitigate ethnic conflicts? and 3) What kind of research would help shed some of the light we need on this subject?

As to the first question — whether ethnic groups have a future in American society — the previous chapters have, I hope, provided sufficient answer. There is no reason to think they will not continue to play an important role, at least for the rest of this century, despite the fact that the compositions of the groups are changing, as well as the kind of identification they provide for their members. (Joshua Fishman, in his large and impressive study of language loyalty,[1] indicates that there is apparently an inevitable decline across generation lines in the use of a foreign tongue, although he and many of his co-authors entertain some hope that the decline can be arrested and even reversed.)

Although immigration has by no means come to an end, and hundreds of thousands of immigrants enter the United States each year, the ratio of immigrants to the total population is obviously much smaller than it was at the turn of the century. And while the new immigrants do provide clients for the hard core of purely ethnic services (especially the press and radio programs identified with the mother tongue), they no longer represent the major focus of concern for most American ethnics.

Poles, Norwegians and Italians, for example, are far more concerned with shaping their future within the American environment than preserving their cultural links with the past. The cultural links are preserved, however, in two fashions — first, by the unconscious

[56]

transmission of role expectations, some rooted in the past and others in the early experience in this country; and second, through a scholarly or artistic interest in the customs of the past. Thus, though the ethnic groups in this country have taken on a life of their own, more or less independent of the national cultures and societies where their roots lie, many of the old links survive, indirectly and undeliberately, or in a highly self-conscious academic fashion.

Again we can see how blurred the picture is and how difficult it is to be confident in the absence of more careful research. The American Irish are different, let us say, from the American Poles in part because they come from different cultural backgrounds, in part because they came to the United States at different times, in part because the two groups have had vastly different experiences in the American society, and in part because there are conscious efforts — at first from an intense determination to survive, and later out of leisurely academic and artistic interests — to keep a lot of the traditions and customs of the past.

The American Irish, I suspect, are only slightly moved by the current Londonderry riots in which Catholics in the north of Ireland have adopted some of the tactics of American blacks in their own civil rights movement. Not long ago, during a visit to a Catholic girls' college in the heartland of America, I noticed a sign on the bulletin board announcing that the Irish Club of the college would shortly hold its monthly meeting. I asked the young lady who was showing me through the college if she belonged to the Irish Club; it turned out that she not only belonged, she was its president. "Peggy," I asked her, "do you know what the six counties are?" She admitted that she did not. "Have you ever heard of the Sinn Fein?" She had not. "Have you ever heard of the Easter rising, or the I.R.A.?" She conceded her ignorance. Finally, I said "Peggy, do you know who Eamon de Valera is?" She brightened. "Isn't he the Jewish man that is the Lord Mayor of Dublin?" she asked.

And yet Peggy is Irish, and proudly so, though she is part of the fourth generation. She might be hard put to say specifically how she differs from her Polish classmates, but the political style of her family, the shape of its commitment to Roman Catholicism, perhaps even its interpretation of the meaning of the good life, are rooted in the Irish past; and even though Peggy later married a boy with a German name (it was all right, her relatives assured me, because his mother was Irish), she continues to be Irish, and I suspect her children will too, no matter what their name happens to be.

Although I never discussed with Peggy her visit to the mother country, I think she must have found it confusing, because the Irish there looked like her relatives and friends, but didn't quite act that way. For one thing, they lacked the drive and enthusiasm, the free-wheeling optimism, even the irreverence of their American counterparts. I, myself, found it rather difficult in the west of Ireland to remember that I was not on the Southwest Side of Chicago. The faces I saw on the streets, and the young people engaged in the song fest in the Bar of the Sacred Heart Hotel (honestly, that was its name) in Salt Hill, County Galway, were the same faces that I knew on the South Side of Chicago, so it was very easy for me to slip into the manner and behavior I used in consorting with the Chicago Irish. But the casual, informal, laughing style which the Chicago Irish expect from their clergy was most disconcerting to the Galway Irish, and they didn't quite know what to make of this strange Yankee priest who kidded with them, refused to take their diffidence seriously and seemed incapable of the reserve that the Irish clergy maintain with their people. (This is obviously a highly ethnocentric version of what happened, making the American Irish look better than the Irish Irish; a clergyman from County Galway visiting my South Side would see the comparison quite differently, I am sure.)

For Jews, the issue of ethnic identity is, it seems to me, even more subtle and complex. The horrifying disaster of the Second World War made most Jews much more explicitly conscious of their background and cultural traditions, and the existence of Israel as a modern nation state embodying these traditions reinforces this consciousness. Thus, while Jews are one of the most thoroughly acculturated groups in American society, they are also

[58]

extremely conscious of their origins and history, and even in the third and fourth generation they make greater efforts to preserve their own culture than any other major immigrant group.

Intermarriage and Identity

Those who doubt that ethnic groups have much of a future usually point to intermarriage as proof that ethnicity is vanishing on the American scene. The truth is, however, that there is almost nothing in the way of detailed literature on ethnic intermarriage except the studies on intermarriage between Jews and gentiles.[2] The only other careful study I know of was done by Harold Abramson, formerly of the National Opinion Research Center and now at the University of Connecticut, in his doctoral dissertation. Abramson is must reading for anyone concerned with the survival of ethnic and religious groups.

In his study[3] (limited to American Catholics who married other American Catholics), Abramson discovered that ethnic intermarriage does, indeed, increase with generation, education and occupational success. He also found, interestingly enough, that it correlates with a higher level of religious practices for Italians and a lower level of religious practice for Irish. It is the devout Italians who intermarry ethnically, and the less devout Irish. Abramson suggests that the reason for this is the much closer link between religion and nationality among the Irish, as compared with the Italians.

But ethnic intermarriage hardly seems to be a random event. A typical ethnic in Abramson's population was some two and one-half times more likely to choose a mate from his own ethnic group than he would if ethnicity were irrelevant in a choice of spouse. Furthermore, even intermarriage seems to take place along certain ethnically predictable lines — that is to say, if someone does marry outside his ethnic group, he is more likely to choose someone from a group considered relatively close to his own. Thus an Irishman, for example, is much more likely to marry a German than a Pole or an Italian.

Abramson's data, which were collected for another purpose, do not supply the answers to two critical questions. First, what sort of ethnic identification, if any, does the new family choose for itself? While there is not much in the way of precise data, impressionistic evidence (reported by Moynihan and Glazer) seems to indicate that a choice of ethnic identity is made either by the spouses themselves or by their children. I remember a conversation with a young woman who was half Irish (of the Protestant variety) and half Jewish, but the Jewish genes were recessive — or so it seemed, especially since she had spent a year in Trinity College in Dublin and had acquired a slight brogue in the process. It was an interesting experience to be told by a person who had a Celtic face and spoke with a brogue that she had finally decided her ethnic identity was Jewish and not Irish. (I will confess that I am just ethnocentric enough to lament the choice, but there are times, though St. Patrick's Day isn't one of them, when I think it's more fun to be Jewish than Irish.)

The second and more complicated question is: Which traits are passed on to which children in an ethnic intermarriage? Let us consider, for example, the apparent political liberalism of the Irish in comparison with the other Catholic groups described in the previous chapter. In a marriage between an Irish male college graduate and a Polish female college graduate, holding all the other variables constant, whose social atitudes are likely to affect the children? Will the father, rather than the mother, prevail because the father is political leader of the family? Will the father influence his sons and the mother her daughters, or will the flow of influence be vice versa? Or will it all cancel out, with the Polish-Irish children assuming positions on social. issues somewhere between those of the two ethnic groups.

Of course we also have no way of knowing whether the social attitudes reported in the previous chapter will survive into the next generation, even in ethnically endogamous marriages. These complicated questions simply underscore how precious little we know about the later stages of acculturation and assimilation. What we do know, however, scarcely justifies the popular assumption that the ethnic groups are disappearing.

But if they are likely to persist, how is society to cope with the problems that ethnicity generates? For it seems to me we must, above all, recognize that ethnic problems are also likely to persist, and that it does little good to lament them or moralize about them. We must also be carefully aware of our own ethnic biases and not permit ourselves the luxury of superior attitudes toward behavior which, if the truth be told, we dislike mostly because it's not the sort of thing "our kind of people" might do. And thirdly, we must be wary of turning correlations into causes. In the last chapter, for example, we described correlations between "Polishness" and certain ethnocentric attitudes. It would be quite easy to make a leap and say that being Polish "causes" the ethnocentric attitudes — and some Polish critics of the data I've discussed have assumed I was making such a leap, even though there were no grounds for such an assumption. There may be something in the Polish cultural background to explain anti-Semitism, but there is nothing I can think of that would explain racism. Thus, I would be much more inclined to see the conflict between the Poles and the blacks in terms of the particular stage in the ethnic assimilation process that the Poles happen to have reached at the time when the black group has become militant. In other words, I am inclined to think we can explain the conflict between the Poles and the blacks almost entirely in economic, social and psychological terms, without having to fall back on cultural traditions at all. And I would go even further and say that unless we recognize the validity of the Polish homeowner's attachment to his home and neighborhood, and the legitimacy of his fear that both of these are threatened, we are in no position to cope with the intense animosity between Poles and blacks over this issue. If our reaction to the fears of black immigration is merely to condemn the prejudice of the Poles or, even worse, merely to describe it as Polish prejudice, we might just as well say nothing at all, because we'll be doing more harm than good.

It is easy enough for liberals, intellectuals and other upper-middle-class types to dismiss the Slavic homeowner's fears as primitive and uneducated, but they are still very real fears and, up to a point, valid. Unless we can find ways to lessen these fears — and I for one do not yet know how this can be done — then there is little ground for expecting that inner racial hatred will decline.

The problem is not much easier with respect to the somewhat less intense controversies separating white ethnic groups, one from another. I have no clear notions of how to cope with an apparent increase in Jewish animosity toward Catholics in recent years or with the antagonism between Irish Catholics and other Catholic groups. I suspect we need intergroup dialogue, cultural exchanges and serious interest in the cultural institutions of those groups with which we are most likely to compete. I am also inclined to think we need leaders who are less demagogic since ethnic groups seem to have a genius for flocking to demagogic leadership. And we must show great self-restraint in attacking the leadership of other groups, even though that leadership is likely to leave itself wide open to such attacks. But having repeated suggestions which must be considered as little more than truisms of intergroup work, I am at a loss as to how to proceed further. We simply do not know enough; not enough data are available, not enough experiments have been done, and all too few theories have been advanced to enable us either to understand what is going on or to prescribe remedies for the pathology we may observe.

It does seem to me, however, that it is essential for political leaders, social planners and influential figures in the ethnic communities to abandon the rather foolish controversy of whether ethnicity is a good thing or a bad thing — particularly since it clearly has both good and bad effects — and settle down to a better understanding of what it means and how we may live with it, not merely tolerably, but fruitfully.

A number of people have made some concrete suggestions for helping to "cool" the tensions among America's ethnic groups. Some try to deal with the problems "where they're at," that is, at

[62]

the actual point of collision. The American Arbitration Association, for example, has organized a new Center for Dispute Settlement which will offer free mediation and arbitration services to help resolve differences between racial and ethnic groups, students and school administrators, landlords and tenants, businessmen and consumers, and other groups involved in clashes that might otherwise escalate into dangerous confrontations.

Others address themselves to efforts to get at the underlying causes. If competition for scarce, or presumably scarce, opportunities and services is at the root of much of the conflict among ethnic groups, they reason, one way to reduce such conflict is to "enlarge the pie" through economic and social programs aimed at improving the overall quality of life for all Americans. Such proposals have come from a variety of sources, including the carefully detailed Freedom Budget, outlined a few years ago by economists Leon Keyserling and Vivian Henderson and others, and the broad *Agenda for the Nation* recently published by the prestigious consultants of the Brookings Institution. All of these proposals envision a shift in national priorities to channel some of our enormous productive capacities into programs to provide jobs, schools, housing, recreation, health services and other essentials, not only for the hard-core poor who, in our less affluent past, have been consistently squeezed out in the competition for these needs, but also for the many millions of hard-working lower-middle-class ethnics embittered by poor schooling, dead-end jobs and an unrelenting, unfair tax burden.

For some years Daniel Patrick Moynihan has railed at the intellectuals, liberals, social workers and other professional "do-gooders" who fail to recognize the realities and deep fears of lower-middle-class and working-class whites. They see their homes and communities being threatened by "outsiders"; and they feel they are being taxed to support the destruction of their own communities by militant non-white groups while the American political elite ignore their problems. "In the present state of race relations and the mounting radicalism of both the left and the right," writes

Moynihan, "it may be argued that what is needed is a program that will benefit everyone, rather than just a few, thereby asserting the unities of the nation, rather than emphasizing those qualities that divide it."[4]

Those of us who are more cosmopolitan are not likely to sink roots as deeply as the members of lower and middle-class white ethnic groups. We therefore do not really understand what a home, a block and a neighborhood mean to such workingmen and their families. To dismiss their fears for the destruction of their neighborhoods by in-migrants of a different race as prejudice may service our need to have a scapegoat for social problems, but it is not a constructive way of facing the problem.

In the words of Irving M. Levine, urban affairs director of the American Jewish Committee:[5]

> In part because of his own powerlessness, in part because of fear, the white workingman sees Negroes as the enemy, especially as they begin to demand, march, riot, and obtain political power. Since the Negro group is also an acceptable symbol of dislike, it is a perfect target for the resentment of a class of rather impotent Americans. By exaggerating the results of Negro aggressiveness, the white worker is saying, "Why doesn't someone speak up for me?"

New Concepts, New Approaches

A few scholars and social activists are beginning to look at the problem in this new way and to devise new strategies for working with ethnic groups. David Danzig of Columbia University, who was one of the first to write about group interests and their potential for intergroup conflict, points out that "only a generation ago, a good deal of the political life of the nation was fashioned in the image of just these [white ethnic] groups." Now, he explains, "ethnic groups are being relegated to a kind of expendable segment of the population."[6]

Danzig and others conclude that new social institutions are needed to replace those that are now obsolete. Once the labor union, the church, and the political club served as intermediate structures between the individual and the complicated, anonymous society around him. There was someone people could tell their troubles to and know that something would be done for them. Today, both churches and unions have become large, bureaucratic organizations, and the political clubs have been replaced by "good government" reformers. In this age of punch cards and electronic switchboards it has become almost impossible to find someone to turn to for comfort.

How, then, can ethnic groups make their needs known? On the Northwest Side of Chicago and in South Philadelphia, both mixed white ethnic neighborhoods, and in an Italian neighborhood in the Bronx, there are new community organizations built around the problems of their members — not merely protectionist groups banding together out of fear and frustration, but people working for better housing, improved recreational facilities, consumer protection and similar needs common to all who live in the neighborhood.

Levine suggests a number of such substantive issues around which ethnic Americans can rally. He points out, for instance, that it has been a mistake to allow the law-and-order issue to become a right-wing battle cry, and he thinks community groups should be encouraged to organize around "shaping a safer neighborhood" just as they have organized around schools, housing and welfare. In place of vigilantism, Levine has in mind developing among fearful groups a recognition of the new possibilities for fighting crime more effectively. Such things as "upgraded police training, sophisticated electronic devices and advanced communications . . . must become the focus of widespread public demand."

Levine and others also urge some measure of tax relief as a response to the frustration that many ethnic Americans feel, and he urges labor, the churches, and the community organizations to press for doubling the $600 dependency allowance and for replacement of local school taxes by a graduated statewide tax. "Surely this is an issue that speaks for the needs of white ethnic America," he says, "and at the same time it may serve to equalize city and suburban school budgets, bringing benefits to black children as well as white taxpayers."

[65]

It is worth noting that Nat Hentoff, anti-establishment writer and social critic, also has picked up this theme: "Those on the Left," he writes, "ought to try to get inside the isolation of those whites making five to ten thousand a year and just hanging on.... 'The average white ethnic male'...needs tax relief, badly, and to get it, he might well join politically in a move to make taxation a good deal more equitable.... If he gets his, he won't be all that bugged about the blacks getting theirs, no matter what he thinks of them."[7]

The cost and quality of education is closely related to taxation, especially in the working-class suburban communities where many ethnic Americans now live. The schools in many of these communities are often woefully inadequate, as are the more deteriorated black schools in the inner cities. It is not altogether surprising that the residents of these communities object to the emphasis on upgrading black schools alone. As Levine points out, "the lower middle class . . . has been made to feel that it is they who must now sacrifice to remedy deficiencies in public education."

Jack Meltzer, of the University of Chicago Urban Studies Program, advocates "a 'Headstart' program to prepare advantaged children to welcome" disadvantaged children into their schools. In a somewhat different vein, Levine argues:

> While equality in education is still a fighting issue, and should occupy our time and conscience, in reality the widespread obsolescence of education is a more inclusive fight. The possibilities opened up by effective decentralization and community participation, by computer technology, and by a widening of the choice of educational options should be disseminated throughout ethnic America and held up as models for new programs. The granting of a per-pupil stipend might encourage new, competing educational systems, relieve the failure-oriented public school apparatus of the total burden and satisfy parents of parochial school children (most of whom are ethnic whites) that their special financial problems are not totally disregarded.[8]

I am forced to comment, in passing, that when an American Jewish Committee staff member can raise the possibility of alternatives to public education — alternatives which would be supported presumably by governmental grants — it is something of an innovation. And, even though the American Jewish Committee remains steadfastly opposed to government aid to religious schools, it should be clear to the reader that one most obvious existing alternative to public education is parochial education — which, incidentally, has an appeal of its own to many ethnic Americans. If one combines these suggestions with Christopher Jencks' call, in *The New York Times Magazine*,[9] for a subsidized private education for black Americans, we have the beginnings of a program which, if it were seriously implemented, would mean a drastic pluralization of American education. There is much irony in these proposals, not the least of which is that they hint at pluralization at the very time that many American Catholics are decrying their own separate school system.

The suggestions described above touch primarily on socioeconomic needs: personal safety, taxes, schools. But those searching for answers to intergroup hostility are aware also of the deep psychological needs for identity, community and belonging. Robert Wood, former Undersecretary of the Department of Housing and Urban Development and now head of the MIT-Harvard Joint Center for Urban Studies, warns that economic aid and a higher standard of living "bring no relief from loneliness and anonymity. The cultivation of group, family, or kind," he says, "is a powerful support [against] the unbearable pressures of urban life."[10]

Levine, too, speaks to the issue of mental health in broader terms than psychiatry and organized treatment institutions. He describes "closed people who are moving in tunnels, frightened of a world where no one seems to be in control — least of all, themselves." And he calls on churches, unions and ethnic societies to undertake new forms of entertainment and leisure-time activities that counteract the inertia of the lower middle class, and to demand new public and private mental health programs, with the kinds of retreats and group settings that would help people open themselves up and deal with their anxieties.

I find myself deeply impressed with the courage and imagination that Levine and the others bring to this issue. The programs they propose will not, by themselves, solve the problem of conflict between blacks and white ethnics. They will not even be launched before many ideological prejudices among white liberals are overcome; but a beginning must be made somewhere, and certainly their suggestions represent the possibility, even the hope, of a brilliant beginning.

The American Jewish Committee is considering a program of local and national consultations to bring together leaders of ethnic groups, educational institutions, religious structures, community-action agencies, mass media, and civic and business organizations to study the implications of the rediscovery of ethnic America for the life of the nation. Out of such consultations, it is hoped, various programs would be developed to help ethnic leaders grapple with the problems of their own groups and of the larger society. Such action models, the Committee suggests, might include: an ethnic coalition committed to reducing intergroup tensions; a labor-supported community-action program for white workers; ethnic and cultural identity programs in mainstream institutions; new forms of fraternal, service and religiously sponsored activities; and projects to promote mass-media consciousness of ethnic America. Each program would be designed to address the problems of ethnic America, and its success would be measured by the degree to which group needs were met and group conflict decreased.

This program grows out of a tradition of coping with group problems in urban situations; it is a sophisticated tradition and one that has had considerable success in the past. Given enough money and enough patience, such approaches could make a major contribution to easing tensions both between black and white and among white groups. However, there is a new variable which must be taken into account, and which may force a drastic rethinking of the traditional model of intergroup work.

The white ethnic groups are no longer immigrant groups. They are no longer poor, depressed, downtrodden and uneducated. But despite a moderate financial and educational achievement, they are still deeply suspicious of "outsiders," particularly when these

[68]

outsiders are "professors" or "intellectuals" or "experts." Presumably the parents and grandparents of these ethnics were also suspicious of outsiders, but lacking economic and educational resources, they were in no position to indulge their suspicions nearly as much as the present generation. The very fact that the ethnics have become acculturated, though not assimilated, will make them more, rather than less, difficult to work with.

It seems to me that it is up to the organized agencies within the ethnic groups to take the lead in cooperation. (I would even propose, for example, that Jewish agencies declare a moratorium on further research on anti-Semitic attitudes and instead find agencies of other ethnic or religio-ethnic groups with which they can cooperate in studying the much larger issue of inter-ethnic animosity. In fact, as a general principle, I think no ethnic agency in the United States ought, at the present time, engage in research by itself, or solely on its own population.)

The Research Gap

I come back now to my own favorite theme — the urgent need for additional research in the entire area of ethnic relations. What sort of research is needed? There isn't *any* demographic socioeconomic or sociopsychological information about the latter stages of the acculturation process of American ethnic groups; it simply does not exist, and it is not likely to exist in the foreseeable future. There's a great likelihood that no attempt will be made to collect such information until it is too late. The Census Bureau now provides data only on the foreign born, and tells us nothing about the second, third, or fourth-generation Americans. If one looks under "Ethnicity" in the indices of the behavioral science journals, one can find articles about Eskimos and Navaho, about tribes in Africa and New Guinea, even occasionally about black-white relationships, but precious little else. Ethnic questions are not routinely included in survey questionnaires, and for all the wild assertions about ethnic voting patterns (based usually on the foreign-born percentages of the Census tract data), national samples of political behavior rarely break down the American religious groups into their various ethnic components.

Even though graduate students are interested in writing dissertations on the subject (a strange application of Hansen's law), the number of faculty members who feel qualified to sponsor such dissertations is virtually nil. The sprightly Glazer and Moynihan book[11] offers interesting data and speculations about New York City, but New York City is not, as startling as it may seem, the whole republic. Herbert Gans' book about the Italians of Boston[12] is extremely suggestive, but one looks in vain for imitators of Gans. Fishman's book on language loyalty is extremely valuable but quite narrow in its focus; it tells us nothing, for example, about ethnic groups like the Irish who speak only English, and that sometimes not too well. Gordon's book[13] is, as far as I know, the only serious attempt to state some general propositions about ethnicity in American society. Yet, anyone who argues that ethnic research is important is told first that the question is quite irrelevant because of the workings of the assimilation process, and second that it is a highly sensitive issue which might offend people if pushed too vigorously. How something can be irrelevant and sensitive, no longer an issue and still offensive, is one of those great paradoxes that we gentlemen adventurer sociologists must learn to live with. One can submit articles on ethnicity to respectable journals and not even expect the courtesy of having the articles rejected, and research proposals to governmental agencies are likely to be dismissed without the formality of a visit from the site committee. Ethnic study is out, and unlikely to come in, in the near future.

I shall not speculate at great length as to the reason for this lack of interest, but one is truly hard put to know why the last serious sociological study of American Poles was done by Thomas and Znaniecki in 1918. It could be, as one middle-aged Ph.D. from Columbia suggested to me, that those who trained the present generation of younger American sociologists repressed the possibility of ethnic research from their consciousness because of their own profound ambivalence about their ethnic backgrounds.

[70]

In my judgment, we must collect a great deal of basic demographic and socioeconomic information which simply does not exist now. We must know who and where and what the major ethnic groups are — not merely the large groups we have spoken of here, but also the smaller groups, which may be even more instructive for understanding a multiple-melting-pot model of society — the Greeks, the Armenians, the Luxembourgers, the Lebanese and others who are still very much with us and from whom there is a lot to be learned. Once we had the basic demographic information, we could go on to attitude and value studies, and the more complicated questions about the impact of ethnicity on social structure. (I say we could because, in all honesty, I don't really believe that we will. In fact, I don't even believe we are going to start putting ethnicity on survey research questionnaires as a standard item.)

Besides collecting basic demographic, socioeconomic and socio-psychological data about the American ethnic groups, I think we must do two other kinds of research: We must support graduate students who are willing to go into the ethnic ghettos that survive in our big cities, and even in our suburbs, and study closely the life styles and the role expectations of those who live in these ethnic communities. (Hopefully, the students will be operating out of the same general theoretical perspective, asking similar questions and periodically comparing notes with each other; unless this is done, we are not going to have the kind of raw material out of which survey questions can be formed to give us precise statistics about the different role expectations of ethnic groups.)

We also need to do case studies of both conflict and cooperation situations, so that we have some idea of what environmental and personal factors can turn competition into cooperation, or at least prevent it from becoming open conflict. I am inclined to suspect that since ethnic animosity is deeply rooted in the personality, psychiatry can make a major contribution to this sort of research.

Let me cite, for example, some very provocative data on Catholic-Jewish relations published last year in a book by Martin Marty,

Stuart Rosenberg and myself.[14] The data are based on two surveys conducted for the *Catholic Digest* — one by the Ben Gaffin firm in 1952, the other by the Gallup organization in 1965 (Table 5).[15]

Table 5. ATTITUDES OF JEWS AND CATHOLICS
TOWARD EACH OTHER, 1952 AND 1965

	Changes in attitudes of			
	Catholics toward Jews		Jews toward Catholics	
	Favorable	Unfavorable	Favorable	Unfavorable
Think "we" are prejudiced against "them"	7%	—	—	15%
Think "they" are prejudiced against "us"	6	—	—	14
They interfere with our liberties	1	—	—	6
They are unfair in business	8	—	2%	—
They are dishonest in public office	5	—	—	8
They don't respect our belief	—	5%	—	10
Would vote for one of them as President	26	—	27	—
They would not want to intermarry with us	17	—	—	17
Employers in their group would discriminate against us	6	—	—	6
They stick together too much	5	—	—	3
They are getting too much power	21	—	6	—
Their clergymen are not intelligent	0	0	—	17
Their clergymen don't promote understanding	3	—	—	17
Their clergymen don't promote civic cooperation	4	—	—	13
Their clergymen don't set a good personal example	1	—	—	5
They try to influence the press	5	—	—	7
Their magazines are not fair	2	—	—	12
Have had unpleasant experience, causing dislike, with one of them	1	—	—	4

The most striking finding of the research is that in the thirteen years covered, there has been a downward shift in unfavorable feelings among Catholics toward Jews in all but two of the measures used, while among Jews unfavorable attitudes toward Catholics have increased in all but three of the measures. (In only one respect had attitudes on both sides improved at the same rate: willingness to vote for a member of the other group as President.)

In 1965, Jews were far more likely than they were in 1952, for example, to say they thought their own group was prejudiced against Catholics and that Catholics were prejudiced against Jews. They were also far more likely to express the feeling that Catholics do not respect Jewish beliefs, that Catholics do not want to intermarry, that Catholic clergy are not intelligent and do not promote understanding, that Catholic magazines are not fair. On five of these seven subjects, the Catholics' attitude toward Jews had become more favorable. Altogether the responses suggest that the two groups have switched places: In 1952, Catholics had a more negative attitude toward Jews than Jews did toward Catholics; by 1965 the reverse seemed to be true.

What is even more troubling is that this apparent increase in anti-Catholic feeling appeared to be concentrated among the younger and the more religious Jews. Moreover, the negative feelings occurred most often among the college-educated; they evidently did not stem from ignorance or lack of sophistication, and could not be counted on to go away in time.

Let me stress that we must be very cautious in interpreting this apparent change in Jewish attitudes toward Catholics. The Jewish sample of 1952 survey was quite small, and though the size of the 1965 survey was large enough to permit some confidence in the accuracy of the data, the findings are nonetheless highly tentative and must be viewed with considerable reservation.

If, however, our sample is representative of the Jewish population, and *if* it continues to be representative when the Jews are divided into educational and age subgroups, then not only is there an increase in anti-Catholic feeling among American Jews, but

[73]

this increase is most marked among college graduates and younger Jews and therefore seems likely to grow worse instead of better.

Indeed, if these phenomena are valid representations of reality, a very notable problem in Catholic-Jewish relationships may be facing us in years to come — particularly when Catholics, whose attitudes toward Jews appear to have improved substantially in the last ten years, discover that the reverse has happened among Jews. Such a discovery might lead to a resurgence of anti-Jewish feeling among Catholics; and the widespread optimism that an era of religious good will in the United States is about to begin may prove unjustified.

Some sociologists have claimed — I think without proper qualification — that among gentiles, particularly Protestants, religiousness is related to anti-Jewish feeling. I am not prepared, on the basis of the data cited above, to say that among Jews religiousness is related to increased anti-Catholic feeling — if indeed there be such an increase. But surely a minimal conclusion from these findings is that considerably more research is necessary on the subject of Catholic-Jewish relationships. Perhaps it also would not be inappropriate to suggest that Catholic and Jewish agencies join together to study the relationships between their two groups, and that it would be a mistake, in view of the findings just cited, to concentrate merely on anti-Jewish feeling among Catholics.

I want to emphasize again that it seems to me all these research efforts ought to be jointly sponsored by a number of ethnic agencies, whether by themselves or in cooperation with foundations and the Federal government. Indeed, research on the research project — that is to say, studies of how ethnic agencies cooperate in research projects — would itself make interesting investigation.

Let me conclude with a story whose point I think I need not elaborate. I was standing in front of a church in the west of Ireland, camera in hand, attempting to record the church which I thought just possibly was the place of my grandfather's baptism. The parish priest who was out cutting his hedge despite the rain, approached me, noted that I was a new man around here, and introduced himself. I must say I was a bit surprised when, on hearing my name, he remarked, "Ah, yes, you'd be the sociologist fellow from Chicago." Then he added, "Would you be wantin' your grandfather's baptismal record now?"

I admitted that the idea hadn't occured to me. He shook his head in discouragement. "Ah," he said, "fine sociologist you are."

"Do a lot of people come seeking such records?" I asked. He nodded gravely.

"Indeed they do," he said, "Indeed they do. Those poor people, you know, they've been in the States now for three generations and they come seeking roots; they want to know who they are; they want to know all about their past and their ancestors. The poor people, I feel so sorry for them. Well," he continued, "the least we can do is to be of some help to them. That's why I had all their baptismal records put on microfilm. It makes it a lot easier for people to find their roots."

NOTES

1. Joshua Fishman *et al.*, *Language Loyalty in the United States* (London and The Hague: Mouton, 1966).

2. Marshall Sklare, "Intermarriage and the Jewish Future," *Commentary*, April 1964, and Erich Rosenthal, "Studies of Jewish Intermarriage in the United States," *American Jewish Year Book*, Vol. 64 (1963), two of the best research reports on this subject.

3. Harold Abramson, unpublished doctoral dissertation, University of Chicago, 1969.

4. *The Reacting Americans: An Interim Look at the White Ethnic Lower Middle Class* (New York: The American Jewish Committee, 1968), p. 25.

5. Irving M. Levine, "A Strategy for White Ethnic America." Paper delivered at Conference on the Problems of White Ethnic America, University of Pennsylvania, June 25, 1968. (The American Jewish Committee.)

6. David Danzig, "The Social Framework of Ethnic Conflict in America." Paper delivered at National Consultation on Ethnic America, Fordham University, June 20, 1968. (The American Jewish Committee.)

7. Nat Hentoff, "Counterpolitics: The Decade Ahead," *Evergreen Review*, February 1969, p. 25.

8. *The Reacting Americans, op. cit.*, p. 27.

9. Christopher Jencks, "Private Schools for Black Children," *The New York Times Magazine*, November 3, 1968, p. 30.

10. *The Reacting Americans, op. cit.*, pp. 7, 14.

11. *Beyond the Melting Pot, op. cit.*

12. *The Urban Villagers, op. cit.*

13. *Assimilation in American Life, op. cit.*

14. Martin Marty, Stuart Rosenberg and Andrew M. Greeley, *What Do We Believe?* (New York: Meredith Press, 1968).

15. This table is borrowed, with some revisions in language and arrangement, from Marty *et al., op. cit.*, p. 174.

Don't miss *these important companion books:*

■ **NOT QUITE AT HOME**
How an American Jewish Community Lives
With Itself and Its Neighbors

BY MARSHALL SKLARE, JOSEPH GREENBLUM AND BENJAMIN B. RINGER
A look beneath the surface of a tranquil upper-middle-class suburb, with
revealing insights into the religious life of Jewish residents, the problems
they face in preserving their Jewishness, and the limits of their relationships with gentiles. A glimpse into the future of Jewish life and identity
in America. **$1.00**

■ **THE SHORTCHANGED CHILDREN OF SUBURBIA**
What Schools Don't Teach About Human Differences
And What Can Be Done About It

BY ALICE MIEL WITH EDWIN KIESTER, JR. How public schools in a typical
American residential community fail to prepare children to live in a
world of many cultures, races, religions and economic levels. Includes
an action program for helping children understand human differences
and develop social and ethical values consonant with our democratic
tradition. **$1.00**

■ **BETTER THAN YOU**
Social Discrimination
Against Minorities in America

BY TERRY MORRIS. How the "ins" have kept the "outs" out, and what is
being done about it. A closeup of clubs that bar Jews, Catholics, blacks,
Puerto Ricans, American Indians; of executive-suite jobs closed to those
who can't join the right clubs; of "gentlemen's agreements" and zoning
laws that keep minority groups out of cooperative apartments and the less
than affluent out of affluent suburbs. **$1.25**

INSTITUTE OF HUMAN RELATIONS PRESS • 165 East 56 Street, New York, N.Y. 10022

MORRIS B. ABRAM, President, Brandeis University: ...crisis is not only a university dilemma but a national problem, this book should help translate the vague thoughts and observations of many of us into substance for debate, reflection — and perhaps solution.

HERBERT J. GANS, Visiting Professor of Sociology, Columbia University: Father Greeley's report is an interesting and provocative statement about the continued role of ethnicity in American life and raises enough questions to keep researchers busy for a generation.

RICHARD GORDON HATCHER, Mayor of Gary: . . . a thoughtful overview of a problem too long ignored. Father Greeley challenges us to examine some of our preconceptions, and suggests interesting lines for further research.

PAUL JENNINGS, President, International Union of Electrical Workers, AFL-CIO-CLC: This publication will make a significant contribution in helping us to identify and understand some of our current social and racial problems.

JOSEPHINE NIEVES, Director Northeast Region, U.S. Office of Economic Opportunity: Father Greeley's scholarly and penetrating study of a vital aspect of American life will serve to reawaken planners to the absolute necessity of considering ethnic qualities in the development of policy and programs.

THOMAS F. PETTIGREW, Professor of Sociology, Harvard University: Father Greeley has written, in his typically direct style, a valuable and insightful contribution toward understanding our multi-ethnic society. His broad and often speculative treatment could well initiate a renewal of research interest in this vital aspect of American life.

CARL B. STOKES, Mayor of Cleveland: This study is a significant contribution to understanding the ethnic diversity of our citizens. Such diversity adds immeasurable richness and strength to urban culture, while at the same time it adds tension and conflict, the threat of which the author seems to fully appreciate.

Eighth Printing
September 1981

36